ROUTER

METHODS OF WORK

The Best Tips from
25 Years of *Fine Woodworking*

ROUTER

METHODS OF WORK

EDITED AND
ILLUSTRATED BY

JIM RICHEY

The Taunton Press

Publisher: Jim Childs
Associate Publisher: Helen Albert
Associate Editor: Strother Purdy
Copy Editor: Suzanne Noel
Indexer: Harriet Hodges
Cover and Interior Designer: Carol Singer
Layout Artist: Karen Healey
Illustrator: Jim Richey

FINE WOODWORKING MAGAZINE
Editor: Timothy D. Schreiner
Art Director: Bob Goodfellow
Managing Editor: Anatole Burkin
Associate Editors: William Duckworth, Matthew Teague,
    Asa Christiana
Copy/Production Editor: Thomas McKenna
Associate Art Director: Michael Pekovich

ABOUT YOUR SAFETY
Working with wood is inherently
dangerous. Using hand or power tools
improperly or ignoring standard safety
practices can lead to permanent injury
or even death. Don't try to perform
operations you learn about here (or
elsewhere) unless you're certain they are
safe for you. If something about an
operation doesn't feel right, don't do it.
Look for another way. We want you to
enjoy the craft, so please keep safety
foremost in your mind whenever you're
working with wood.

Taunton
BOOKS & VIDEOS

for fellow enthusiasts

Printed in the United States of America
10 9 8 7 6 5 4 3 2 1

The Taunton Press, Inc.,
63 South Main Street, PO Box 5506,
Newtown, CT 06470-5506
e-mail: tp@taunton.com

Distributed by Publishers Group West

Library of Congress Cataloging-in-Publication Data
Router : methods of work / edited and illustrated by Jim Richey.
        p.   cm.
    "The best tips from 25 years of Fine Woodworking."
    Includes index.
    ISBN 1-56158-369-3
        1. Routers (Tools). 2. Joinery. 3. Jigs and fixtures. I. Richey, Jim.
    II. Fine woodworking.
    TT203.5.R67   2000
    684'.083—dc21   00-037392

ACKNOWLEDGMENTS

MAKING GOOD MAGAZINE COLUMNS and books is not a solitary endeavor—it requires collaboration of the finest kind. Twenty-some years ago John Kelsey took a chance on me—thanks, John. My deepest gratitude goes to the magazine staff members I've worked with over the years: Rick Mastelli, Jim Cummins, Jim Boesel, Alec Waters, and Bill Duckworth. These guys did most of the hard work and didn't get much of the credit. I'd like also to recognize art directors Roland Wolf and Bob Goodfellow for their gentle and perceptive coaching. I am also most grateful for Strother Purdy's help and support in putting together this series of books.

But most important, I would like to thank the hundreds of woodworkers whose creative ideas and clever tricks are represented here. We couldn't have done it without you.

CONTENTS

Introduction *2*

Chapter 1
ROUTER SETUP AND MAINTENANCE *4*

Chapter 2
ROUTER TABLES AND MOUNTS *32*

Chapter 3
BASES AND ALIGNMENT FIXTURES *56*

Chapter 4
ROUTING DADOES *72*

Chapter 5
ROUTING DOVETAILS *90*

Chapter 6

ROUTING MORTISES AND CAVITIES *110*

Chapter 7

ROUTER JOINERY *128*

Chapter 8

FIXTURES FOR CURVED AND
CIRCULAR WORK *154*

Chapter 9

FLUTING, REEDING
AND MILLING *172*

Chapter 10

ROUTER METHODS
AND ODD JOBS *194*

Index *232*

INTRODUCTION

 IN PUTTING TOGETHER THIS BOOK I was surprised to find out that the first portable electric router was manufactured in 1905 by the Kelly Electric Machine Co. of Buffalo, New York. Surprised, because I worked as a carpenter for several years in the 1960s, and I would have sworn the router came out of nowhere and into general usage during that time frame. Regardless, this versatile Swiss army knife of the woodworking world is now found in nearly every woodworker's shop in the world and, for many, is the first power woodworking tool they own.

Right out of the box you can put a router to work routing dadoes, shaping the edges of boards, cutting circles and making signs. Or you can mount it upside down in a table to perform even more tricks. In many woodworkers' shops a router table is the place where door panels are shaped and trim is made—territories that were once the exclusive domain of the shaper.

But underneath it all the router is a simple tool—basically just a high rpm motor with a chuck on one end. It is this simplicity (or so goes my thesis) that inspires woodworkers to apply the router for creative solutions to nonstandard problems. And over the years readers of the Methods of Work and Q&A columns of *Fine Woodworking* magazine have been abundantly inspired—inventing and contributing hundreds of router-based solutions. We combed through 25 years' worth of these solutions and collected the best here in one book. You will learn how to mill a giant sphere, flatten a workbench top, make a gymnastics balance beam or mill dollhouse siding. You will find dozens of special router bases, jigs and fixtures—one for almost every conceivable woodworking situation.

In short, if you're looking for new tricks to teach your router, here's the place.

[*Chapter 1*]

ROUTER
SETUP &
MAINTENANCE

Selecting the Right Bit for Template-Routing

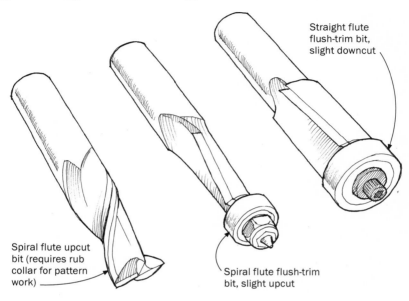

Straight flute
flush-trim bit,
slight downcut

Spiral flute upcut
bit (requires rub
collar for pattern
work)

Spiral flute flush-trim
bit, slight upcut

H ERE ARE SOME THINGS to consider when choosing a router bit
for template-routing. The first decision you must make is between a flush-trimming bit (which has a built-in ball bearing to follow
the template) or a standard router bit (which requires the use of a rub
collar to follow the template). Let's start with flush-trimming, or
pattern-cutting, bits. These range in diameter from ¼ in. to 1¼ in., and
in general you should use the largest-diameter bit that is comfortable
for you and your router. A large-diameter bit presents a shallower
angle of attack to the workpiece, thereby reducing or eliminating
tearout. However, a large bit may be intimidating to you and present
runout problems for your router.

The amount of stock you are removing with a given diameter bit will also affect your cut quality. In general, on ¾-in. and thicker stock, don't cut more than 25% of your bit's diameter from the edge of the workpiece per pass. For example, a ½-in.-dia. bit is limited to removing ⅛ in. per pass, while a 1-in.-dia. bit can take ¼ in. per pass.

Grain direction also plays a part in cut quality. Feeding against the grain or changing from cutting end grain to edge grain can cause tearout, which can be reduced by using a large-diameter bit.

In general, spiral flute bits slice through the wood cleaner and with less tearout than a comparable-diameter bit with straight flutes. For the cleanest cuts in difficult cutting situations, such as delicate veneers, I recommend spiral flutes over straight flutes. In the size range of bits used for template-routing, three-fluted bits don't have much advantage over two-fluted bits because tip speed is not a major concern. I'd opt for the less expensive two-fluted bits.

For template-routing with a rub collar I'd recommend a spiral-flute upcut bit over a straight-flute bit.

—BRAD WITT, *Davenport, Iowa,*
from a question by Leon Segal, Randolph, N.J.

Are High-Speed Steel Router Bits Better?

S OME WOODWORKERS HOLD that router bits made of high-speed
steel cut more smoothly, sharpen with conventional techniques
and are cheaper than carbide-tipped bits. My opinion is that, other
than being cheaper, there is no real advantage to using high-speed
steel (HSS) bits over carbide-tipped bits. While it is true that HSS
router bits may be ground a little sharper than carbide-tipped bits, this
edge advantage lasts for only a short time. Studies by router-bit manufacturing companies, such as Onsrud, have revealed that the initial
sharpness of an HSS edge deteriorated quickly during cutting; the bit
maintains a lower level of sharpness for the remaining 95% of its life.

As for resharpening router bits by hand, this can be done with both
high-speed steel and carbide-tipped bits by using a diamond honing
stone, such as the Eze-Lap (available from Woodcraft, P.O. Box 1686,
Parkersburg, W.V. 26102; 800-225-1153). However, when sharpening any
high-speed rotating tool, such as a router bit, there is a danger of changing the symmetry of the cutting edges. This can not only unbalance the
bit but also cause only one edge to do the cutting. If one edge sticks
out more than the other, you'll have to reduce the feed rate to get the
same quality of cut as if both edges were cutting equally.

Finally, I don't know where HSS router bits can be purchased
in any great variety. In contrast, carbide-tipped bits appear to be
universally available and are used almost exclusively by professional
woodworkers.

—JERRY GLASER, *Torrance, Calif.,*
from a question by Harry Rudin, Oberrieden, Switzerland

Titanium-Nitride-Coated Router Bits

RECENTLY, SEVERAL ROUTER-BIT manufacturers have started selling router bits, shaper cutters and industrial-quality woodworking cutting tools coated with titanium nitride. The cutting edges and surfaces of these bits have a characteristic golden color. The primary advantage of such a coating is to increase the lubricity of the cutter, which makes chips and sawdust less likely to accumulate. This helps the cutting edge to run cooler, thus increasing the useful life of the edge before resharpening is necessary. Some manufacturers claim the coating increases edge life 5 to 10 times more than a noncoated, high-speed steel edge.

Most titanium-nitride-coated bit users that I've spoken to agree that the coating does increase edge life considerably; therefore, I think the coating is probably worth the added expense, especially on bits that are hard to sharpen because of their complex profile (intricate molding cutters, for example) or on bits used for router mortising, which tend to dull quickly in heavy use. However, in a production shop where a cutter is used all day long, it would probably be best to stick with carbide-tip or solid-carbide bits and cutters, which stay sharp longer than titanium-nitride-coated bits.

—MARK DUGINSKE, *Wausau, Wisc.,*
from a question by Charles R. Draney, Seattle, Wash.

When to Resharpen Carbide Router Bits

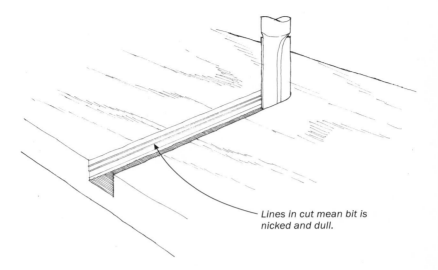

Lines in cut mean bit is
nicked and dull.

T HE FIRST SIGN that a carbide bit needs resharpening is that it's
harder to push the router through a typical cut than it was previously, and the motor will sound like it's straining.

The second thing to check is the quality of the cut. A dull bit will
usually (though not always) have a few ugly nicks in it that leave
bumps on the cut. A dull bit may also burn the plywood.

Carbide router bits were developed for cutting sheet goods with a
high adhesive content. For that reason, the bits will hold up for a long
time before they need sharpening. Bits used only occasionally may
never need sharpening.

When they do, send them out to be sharpened professionally. It's
conceivable that you could sharpen the flutes with a diamond stone
(other stones aren't hard enough), but the carbide is still so hard that

you'd have trouble getting a sharp edge. Professional sharpening services have tooling made for the purpose. In the end, however, it may be cheaper to throw an inexpensive bit away and simply buy another one.

Care when using the bits will help them last longer. Woods with high mineral content, like teak, will dull cutters faster than other woods. If you're routing plywood edges and you have a lot to do, move the bit up or down slightly after cutting a few hundred feet. Glue dulls carbide faster than wood, so if the same section of the bit is always hitting the glue line, you'll wear away the carbide prematurely and soon have little nicks in the edge.

Finally, the manufacturing quality of the bit has much to do with how long it stays sharp. Though many factors are involved, the most important is the quality of the grind. Rough grinding leaves a jagged, serrated edge that will dull quickly. A fine grinding will create a clean edge that will hold up longer. Inspect the edge of the flutes on a new bit before buying it. If a pencil tip scrapes along its edge, rather than slides, the grind is on the rough side.

—JEFF GREEF, *Davenport, Calif.,*
from a question by Theodore Fitzgerald, Clayton, N.C.

What Speed for Large Router Bits?

I F YOU'RE USING LARGE-DIAMETER BITS, such as those 3-in. bits for raising panels, you should definitely run your router at a much slower speed than its maximum rpm. Imagine a ½-in. shank bit with a 3-in. cutting diameter spinning at 25,000 rpm. At the edge of the ½-in. shank, the bit is spinning at approximately 37 mph. But at the very edge, the bit is moving at approximately 223 mph. Heat buildup at the cutting edge is significant, which can burn the cut and the bit, leading to carbide chipping or worse.

Shapers regularly use wide-diameter bits, but they're run at low speeds to keep down the speed at the edge of the bit (the rim speed). This allows for safer and cooler cutting. Shapers are also designed to run continuously at this speed.

A router motor doesn't have the same stamina that a shaper motor has. Running a wide-diameter bit puts a great deal of stress on a router's motor and collet. At high speeds, there's a greater risk of one of these bits vibrating loose and causing damage to the bit, collet, bearings and any and all objects in its flight path. If your router is a variable-speed model, crank the speed control down to its lowest setting, especially when you start it up. If you don't have a variable-speed router, then you can buy a speed-control unit from many of the woodworking-supply companies. These units work much like a light-dimming switch. Most bit manufacturers recommend bit speeds for large-diameter bits. With a 3-in. bit in your router, 10,000 rpm to 12,000 rpm is a much safer speed.

—GARY ROGOWSKI, *Portland, Ore.,*
from a question by Karl Gaffte, Aiken, S.C.

Storing Router Bits

T HIS SIMPLE ROUTER-BIT STORAGE RACK will hold your bits
securely and keep them from falling out or rattling against each
other. The rack is made from a sheet of ⅛-in.-thick Plexiglas and wire
grommets. Wire grommets are rubber, donutlike rings available at auto
parts stores in a variety of sizes; take a router bit with you so you can
buy the size that fits just right.

To make the rack, select a drill bit the same size as the core diameter of the grommet. Drill holes in the Plexiglas at 1-in. to 2-in. inter-
vals and install a grommet in each hole. Installation will be easier if
you lubricate the skirt of the grommet with a drop of oil.

—DAVID MCCAMPBELL, *Salmon, Idaho*

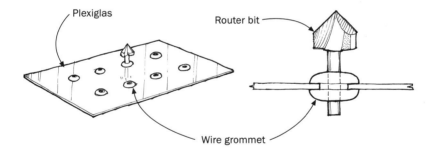

Plexiglas

Router bit

Wire grommet

Under-Bench Router-Storage Drawer

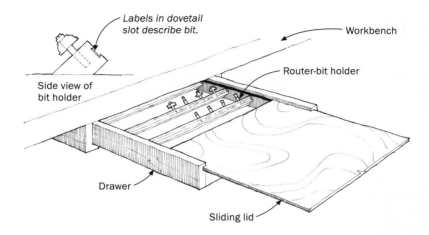

Labels in dovetail slot describe bit.

Workbench

Router-bit holder

Side view of bit holder

Drawer

Sliding lid

S PACE IS AT A PREMIUM in my garage shop. So I built this router-bit storage drawer that fits under my workbench. Make the case from ¾-in. stock with routed slots to accept the bottom and the sliding lid. Cut the bit-holder strips at a 45° angle on the bottom edge, and rout the top face of each strip with a ½-in. dovetail bit to hold labels describing each bit. The labels can include bit size and type (½-in. rounding-over, for example). The case is supported when partially withdrawn, or you can remove it completely for bit selection.

This storage system has been so effective that I added another drawer under the bench to store files.

—BOB BOWLES, *Oxnard, Calif.*

Router Storage in Floral Designer's Foam

FLORAL DESIGNER'S FOAM, the stiff, green material they use to arrange flowers, makes a great storage system for router bits. Simply cut a block whatever size you want and press the shafts of the bits into the block. The holes are clean, and this material seems to prevent rust on the shafts of the bits.

—JEFFREY N. SALES, *Tucson, Ariz.*

Shaving Your Router Bit

WHEN PITCH AND CRUD BUILDS UP on the cutting edge of your router bit, simply shave the buildup off with a disposable razor, and then wipe the bits clean with turpentine. If you do this each time you use your router, you'll get cleaner cuts and prolong the life of your bits.

—WELLS MASON, *Austin, Tex.*

Preventing Router Bits
from Slipping in the Collet

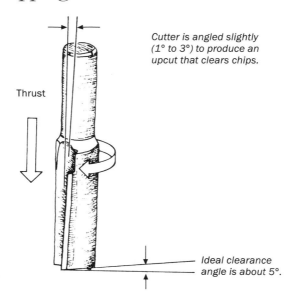

Cutter is angled slightly
(1° to 3°) to produce an
upcut that clears chips.

Thrust

Ideal clearance
angle is about 5°.

SOME WOODWORKERS find that, when setting their router to make a deep, hogging cut in a tough wood like oak, the bit slips down in the collet slightly during the cut, ruining the workpiece. Here's why this happens and how to prevent it.

To clear waste from the cut, some (not all) router bits have cutters brazed on at a slight angle to the bit axis, as in the drawing. This angle creates an upcut that lifts chips out of the cut much as an auger would. Under the heavy load of hogging, this upcut exerts considerable downward thrust on the bit, actually pulling it out of the collet. The deeper the cut is, the greater the thrust will be. The clearance angle of the bottom of the bit, necessary for plunge-cutting, is critical in countering some of this downward thrust. Too great an angle, more than about 7°, results in a bit that plunges too easily and thus offers little resistance to downward thrust. Tests we've done at Milwaukee Electric Tool Corp. indicate that 5° seems to be the ideal clearance angle.

The easiest way to avoid slippage is to do your deep routing in several shallow passes instead of one deep one. The bit will stay cooler and you'll get a smoother cut. If you must take deep cuts, try to have the bit's clearance angle reduced at the next sharpening. Don't, however, overtighten the collet nut to counter slippage; you risk stripping it or cracking the collet itself. Dirt or chips in the collet seat will keep the collet from gripping the bit evenly, so keep it and the bit shank clean. When you install the bit, push it into the collet until it bottoms and then back it out about ⅛ in. This keeps the bit from vibrating against the unmachined bottom of the seat.

JOHN RUSHMER, *Milwaukee Electric Tool Corp.,*
from a question by W. B. Lord, New York, N.Y.

Cleaning a Rusted Collet

A RUSTY ROUTER COLLET will make bit removal difficult. Here's how to clean your collet without damaging it.

First, be aware that if you remove too much metal when attempting to clean a rusty collet, the collet may not seat properly in the router. And a loose or poorly fitting collet can cause bits to spin off center or loosen during the cut. If you suspect that rust has compromised your collet, replace it. In industry, collets are replaced periodically as a matter of course—not a bad idea for frequent router users as well.

To clean a rusty collet that is otherwise in good shape, use a nylon abrasive pad like Scotch-Brite or steel wool. Don't use sandpaper or emery cloth; they will remove solid metal along with the rust.

Apply oil or grease to the collet (the type is not important), and then wipe it all off. What remains will fill the pores and help prevent new rust from forming. Don't try to prevent rust by coating the collet with lacquer or any other coating. The collet must seat snugly in the router, metal on metal, to be safe and effective.

Always remove the collet from the router spindle when changing bits, and clean out any chips, dirt or other debris before seating the next bit. This will ensure that the bit is as centered as the machining on the router and bit allows.

—JEFF GREEF, *Soquel, Calif.,*
from a question by Andrew Westerhaus, Burnsville, Minn.

Cleaning Router Bits with Baking Soda

T HE MILDLY ABRASIVE NATURE of baking soda can be useful in the shop. Mix the soda with water to form a thick paste that will clean router bits, sawblades and saw tables. Scrub the item with the paste, wipe away the residue and then dry and buff.

—R. B. HIMES, *Vienna, Ohio*

Truing Up the Router Base

M ANY ROUTER BASES ARE ALMOST, but not quite, concentric with the collet center. This has the undesirable effect of varying the distance between the fence and the bit or slightly changing the depth of cut when the router is rotated. You can true up a base by first mounting a short length of straight steel rod in the router. Then drill a rod-sized hole in a flat block of wood, so you can pivot the router in the block with the router base's edge against a disk sander. Clamp the block to the disk-sander table (set at 90°); then rotate the router to sand the base round.

—BILL WEBSTER, *Chillicothe, Ill.*

Two Quick Router Centering Setups

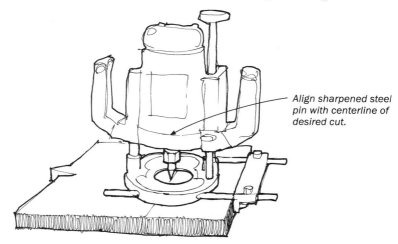

Align sharpened steel pin with centerline of desired cut.

HERE IS A QUICK PROCEDURE for setting the fence on your router. Grind a center point on the end of a steel dowel pin that fits the chuck of your router. You can grind the point by chucking the pin in an electric hand drill, turning on the drill and holding it against a running bench grinder. To use the pointed pin, insert it in the router collet and place the pin right on the centerline of the cut. Then set the fence, replace the pin with the bit, and you're ready to go.

—JEFF TRENTINI, *La Mirada, Calif.*

TO CENTER THE BIT when cutting a mortise with a router, chuck a V-grooving bit in the router (you could substitute an old drill bit ground to a point). With a pointed bit in the router, it's easy to adjust the router's fence so that the bit is over the centerline on the stock. Now remove the centering bit, replace with the mortise bit and rout the mortise dead center.

—DAVID V. NICHOLSON, *Vancouver, B.C.*

Pinpointing Router-Mount and Insert Locations

HERE'S A SIMPLE METHOD to mark the drill holes for mounting a router to a jig or router-table insert. For each threaded mounting hole in the router base, purchase a 1½-in.-long machine screw. Install each machine screw in a drill press with the screw head down. Set the drill press to a slow speed, and use the edge of a flat file to remove the head of the screw and create a centered point. Use this same process to make an end mill for the collet using the unthreaded section of a ¼-in. bolt. Screw in the threaded inserts, points down, and chuck the end mill into the collet, adjusting its height to match that of the threaded inserts. Now carefully place your router on the router-table insert, and press down. The collet and all the threaded inserts will leave a mark pinpointing the exact drill sites.

—MIKE MULLIN, *Manhattan Beach, Calif.*

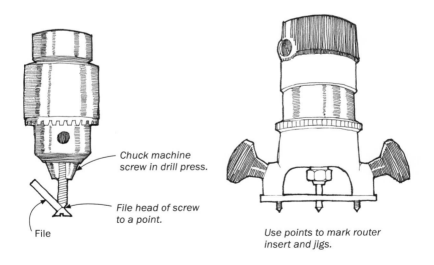

Chuck machine screw in drill press.

File head of screw to a point.

File

Use points to mark router insert and jigs.

Can a Router Substitute for a Shaper?

SOME WOODWORKERS CONSIDER mounting a big router upside down in a table an adequate substitute for a shaper. Not me. I don't believe that you can get the overall equivalent results from a 20-lb. router that you can from a 300-lb. to 400-lb. shaper. Even though the horsepower ratings may be the same, you can't equate the service of a 3-hp router motor with the 80-lb. behemoth that drives Delta's heavy-duty shaper. Also, technicians for several of the companies manufacturing the larger routers say they don't think the routers can take the stress of powering large shaper-type cutters. They fear this stress will destroy the bearings and the resultant heat buildup will cause motor components to fail.

There also are some very important safety considerations. Spindle speeds on a shaper run from 5,000 rpm to 10,000 rpm. A router runs between 20,000 rpm and 25,000 rpm. Centrifugal forces are squared by an increase of rpm. That is, if the rpm is increased from 5,000 to 20,000 (by a factor of 4), the force is increased by a factor of 16. Make sure your bits can stand the strain. Some panel-raising bits are 4 in. in diameter and weigh more than 6 oz. A standard ⅜-in. carbide round-over bit with a pilot bearing weighs less than 1½ oz. and is 1¼ in. in diameter. A large bit has a tendency to grab the stock, possibly dragging the operator's hands into the cutter.

I think you can get some shaper-like functions with a router, especially if you have specific and limited applications in mind. For example, I use a lock-miter bit in limited drawer production and classroom work. I use it in a handheld router with a special jig, and the results are reasonably good and fairly predictable. You won't get true shaper performance and all its possibilities, however, unless you get a machine specifically designed for the purpose.

—BERNARD MASS, *Edinboro, Pa.,*
from a question by Ronald Frey, Clay, N.Y.

Using Shaper Cutters on the Router?

WOODWORKING CATALOGS have been offering a "router adapter," a ½-in. shaft that fits into the router chuck and allows shaper cutters to be used with a router table. Certainly being able to use the huge variety of available shaper cutters on the router table seems like a great idea. But shaper cutters are designed to run between 6,000 rpm and 10,000 rpm, while most variable-speed routers I've seen only go down to about 12,000 rpm at their lowest speed setting. And even though some variable-speed routers, like the Porter-Cable model 7539, are capable of running at 10,000 rpm (the upper limit for most shaper cutters), there's still a chance that you might accidentally forget to select the slowest speed before switching on the router—a very dangerous possibility. Another potential problem is that regular router bits are balanced with shaft and cutting flutes as a single unit. Although a router-adapter shaft may be well balanced and a shaper cutter may be well balanced, the combination of the two may not have proper dynamic balance for safe use.

As a rule, it's best to use router bits in routers and to use shaper cutters in shapers. The two are really quite different machines and require different areas of expertise to set up and to use safely.

—MARK DUGINSKE, *Wausau, Wisc.,*
from a question by Larry A. Keinath, Havertown, Pa.

Makeshift Plunge Routing

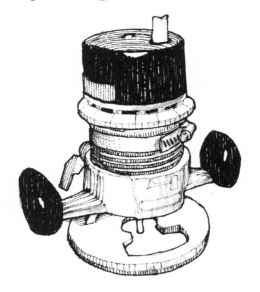

Y OU CAN ADAPT a standard router with a screw-lowering mechanism to allow it to make plunge cuts. Fasten a hose clamp
around the waist of the motor housing to stop the plunge cut at the
desired depth. Loosen the router's tightening cam halfway and spray
inside the base with Teflon lubricant.

—JAMES GENTRY, *Madison, Wisc.*

Vacuum Attachment for the Router

ROUTING PRODUCES a lot of dust and chips. It is much more efficient to collect this messy waste as it is produced rather than to sweep it up later. This sketch shows how I adapted my Sears router to hold my shop-vacuum nozzle.

I positioned the nozzle so that it filled the gap near the router's work light. It's supported in place with a wooden block (screwed to the base) and a steel band. To reduce air leakage through the holes in the router base, I added a solid baseplate made from ¼-in. clear Plexiglas.

—HARRY M. McCULLY, *Allegany, N.Y.*

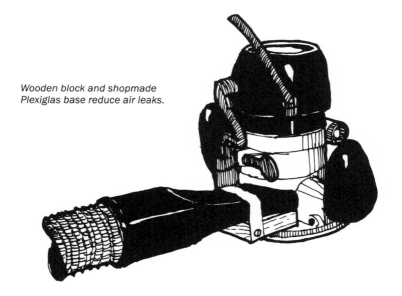

Wooden block and shopmade
Plexiglas base reduce air leaks.

Using Drill-Bit Shanks As Depth Gauges

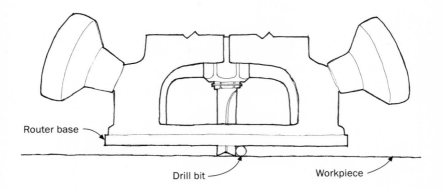

Router base

Drill bit

Workpiece

T WIST-DRILL-BIT DIAMETERS are exact, so a drill laid on its side can be used to set a plunge router to an accurate depth. Put the bit on a flat surface, rest the router base on it, extend the cutter to touch the surface and lock the depth stop.

—PERCY BLANDFORD, *Stratford, England*

Excessive Tearout in Pine

W HEN ROUNDING OVER THE EDGES of pine toy parts, a common problem is excessive tearout. Because pine is a softwood, you will always get a certain amount of tearout, but it can be reduced in the following ways: 1. Buy high-quality carbide bits. The carbide in a good bit can be ground sharper and will hold an edge longer than cheap carbide bits. 2. Try using a router that turns at higher rpms. The faster the revolutions the better the cut. 3. Make sure the bearings in your router are in top shape. Worn bearings let the bit wobble, resulting in a poor cut with more tearout.

To clean up tearout, try power-sanding techniques like vibrator sanders, belt sanders and flap-wheel sanders. The ultimate solution might be to use a different species of wood with better characteristics for toymaking, for example, beech, birch or maple.

—DAVID RUDOLPH, *Santa Barbara, Calif.,*
from a question by R. Hammond, Mississauga, Ont., Canada

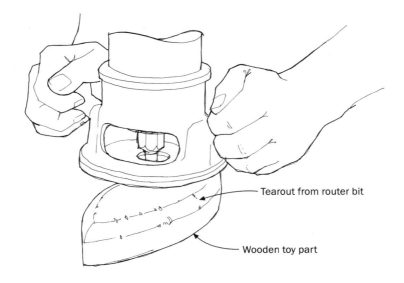

Tearout from router bit

Wooden toy part

Preventing Router Bits from Burning Wood

R ECENTLY A WOODWORKER DESCRIBED this router-caused burning incident. He was routing a ¾-in.-wide, 1¼-in.-deep dado in
mahogany. After routing about half the dado, he smelled wood burning,
yet the dado was clean with no sign of scorching. The sawdust, however,
looked like it had been sprinkled with black pepper. Several spots about
¹⁄₁₆ in. to ⅛ in. dia. began to glow, so he rushed to get a pan of water,
which took about 45 seconds. When he returned, the spots were glow-
ing rings about the size of a quarter. The water quenched the burning
sawdust, but he was shaken by the thought of what could have happened. As for the router bit, only the tip of one edge was a little brown.

When he asked what happened I explained that several things can
cause burning with a router bit. A dull bit causes friction as it rubs
against the wood because the cutting tip is rounded and no longer
shaves a clean slice. This is more common with steel bits, though, than
with carbide.

Moving too slowly through the wood—even if the bit is sharp—
can also cause burning because the bit has time to heat the wood to
its burning point. Last, if you try to take too deep a cut, chips may
clog around the bit and heat up as they rub against each other, the bit
and the wood. Burning is a possibility.

I would only rout a ¼-in.-deep, ¾-in.-wide dado or groove in one
pass with a 3-hp router. A router this powerful will let you plow
through the wood at a speed that will avoid burning. Even so, when
making such cuts, it's best to make them in several passes or to hog
out the bulk first with a dado cutter on the table saw. Plow the dado
on the table saw to within ¹⁄₁₆ in. of its final depth, and then use a
sharp router bit to clean up the cut and take it to depth.

—JEFF GREEF, *Davenport, Calif.,*
from a question by Frederick Eckart, Hatley, Wisc.

Getting Routed Dovetails to Fit Right

WHEN TEMPLATE-ROUTED DOVETAILS don't fit (too loose or too tight), the depth of cut is probably wrong. Depth of cut is critical to a proper fit in routed dovetails. Deepening the cut tightens the joint, while making a shallower cut loosens it. The precise distance from the toe of the cutter to the base of the router depends upon the thickness of the finger template you're using, and the setting recommended by the manufacturer must be taken as an approximation of the exact setting that you determine through experimentation. Raise and lower the bit in ¹⁄₁₆-in. increments until you achieve the desired fit, and then gauge the distance from the toe of the bit to the base of the router. Record this measurement or make a permanent mark on your steel rule. Depending on the wood you're working with, this setting will vary slightly, and it's a good idea to make test cuts on scrap.

If your router is the kind with a rack-gear elevating mechanism, you'll probably have trouble adjusting it with the close precision that's required to cut good dovetails. This trouble is because the depth of cut changes when you tighten the thumbscrew that locks the router motor to its base. The solution is to measure the toe-to-base distance after tightening the thumbscrew; a trial-and-error method to be sure but one that works well with practice.

—*FINE WOODWORKING* EDITORS,
from a question by Jon Gullett, Washington, Ill.

Setting the Dovetail Guide Bushing Accurately on a Sears Router

QUITE BY ACCIDENT, I discovered why I was having trouble cutting accurate dovetails with my Sears router. The three screws holding the plastic router subbase to the rest of the unit are not countersunk, and the base therefore will not be accurately centered with the spindle each time it's removed and replaced.

To correct this, the bit and guide bushing should be installed according to the owner's manual. Then with the router resting on its top, loosen the three base screws. With the lock knob fairly tight (not so tight as to stop vertical movement), lower the cone-shaped dovetail bit until its edges make uniform circumferential contact with the inner edge of the guide bushing, which can be moved about to accomplish this. Rotating the shaft will automatically center the base.

—JAMES L. CAMPBELL, *Orlando, Fla.*

Cleaning a Router Collet with a Gun-Cleaning Kit

A CLEAN COLLET is an absolute must to avoid the disastrous consequences of a router bit slipping up or down in the collet when routing. A gun-cleaning kit for a 22-caliber weapon has everything you need: a small brass brush and patch-cleaning swabs that fit just right in the collet.

—L. D. FREDERICK, *Aspen, Colo.*

Waxing Your Collet

IF YOUR ¼-IN. SPLIT-RING ROUTER COLLET STICKS, making bit removal difficult, apply a thin film of paste wax to the outside surface.

—STEVE SPOLTMAN, *Dayton, Ohio*

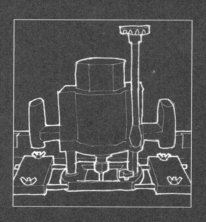

[*Chapter 2*]

ROUTER TABLES
& MOUNTS

Combination Router Table and Outfeed Support

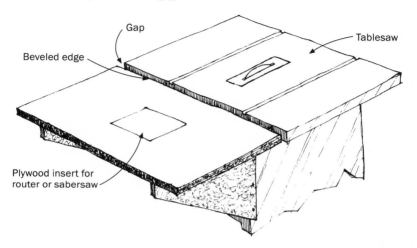

Gap

Tablesaw

Beveled edge

Plywood insert for
router or sabersaw

M Y SHOP IS TOO SMALL to endure much more big equipment. So when I needed both a router table and additional outfeed support on my tablesaw, I combined both functions in the extension table shown in the sketch. Since the table is bolted to the saw, alignment between extension and saw table is better and the table is easy to clean under.

I made the ¾-in. medium-density fiberboard (MDF) table 32 in. wide. Added to the saw table, this gives 44 in. of support. Leave a gap between the saw table and extension so that a plywood panel can be ripped, then crosscut with a sabersaw or circular saw without moving the panel off the table. The blade will travel between saw table and extension. Bevel the front edge of the table so it won't catch work as it leaves the saw table. Cut a 10-in.-sq. hole in the middle of the outfeed table to hold a router or sabersaw mounted on 10-in. plywood inserts. Cut another insert blank to fill the hole when not in use.

—W. DAVID SMOOT, *Duncanville, Tex.*

Router-Table Extension Wing for the Tablesaw

B Y MOUNTING A ROUTER TABLE to the side of the tablesaw as shown, you can combine the control of the saw's miter gauge and rip fence with the safe, crisp cuts of the router. You'll find the saw's miter gauge useful in cutting cross-grain dadoes, dovetails and finger joints. Cut mortises, tenons and with-grain grooves using the saw's rip fence. The combination saves shop space and increases the surface area of your tablesaw. There's never a need to remove the router table—just lower the bit when not in use.

—MARK DUGINSKE, *Wausau, Wisc.*

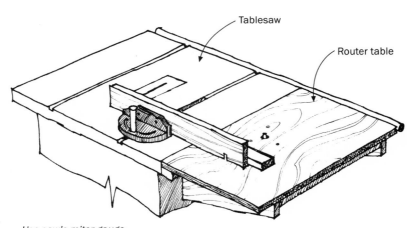

Tablesaw

Router table

Use saw's miter gauge and rip fence.

Removable Router-Table Attachment for Tablesaw

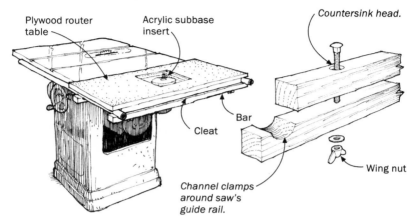

Plywood router table

Acrylic subbase insert

Countersink head.

Bar

Cleat

Wing nut

Channel clamps around saw's guide rail.

W HEN I BEGAN THINKING about a router table, it soon became apparent that finding a home for a large, occasionally used table would be a problem in my crowded basement shop. Finally, it occurred to me while looking at the rip-fence bars extending from my tablesaw that here was an ideal support system for the router table. In addition, I am able to use the saw's fence and miter gauge for certain operations on the router table.

I cut a piece of ¾-in. plywood, 16 in. wide and long enough to fit over the bars. Into this, I routed a ledge to accept an acrylic router subbase. I attached wooden cleats to the bottom of the plywood tightly between the bars to prevent front-to-back movement of the table. A second set of cleats, along with bolts and wing nuts, clamps the table to the bars.

Although the router-table top extends above the saw-table top, limiting the fence travel to the extreme right of the saw table, the saw can still be used for quite a bit of work with the table in place. When necessary, it takes only a minute to remove the table and hang it against the wall.

—MARTIN GINGRICH, *Palmyra, Pa.*

Combination Horizontal and Vertical Router Table

I MADE THIS COMBINATION ROUTER TABLE so that I could quickly switch the tool from the traditional vertical position to a horizontal position for making raised panels and sliding dovetails. The basic concept behind the table is the demountable, ¾-in. plywood, L-shaped router carrier, which has mating sets of mounting holes on each leg of the L. One set of the mounting holes are slotted so that the router may be adjusted up and down in the horizontal position. In the vertical position, the slotted holes allow in/out adjustment of the router's fence. Note that the fence, which normally faces the long end of the table, can be reversed to face the short end of the table for small pieces.

—ANDREW WESTERHAUS, *Burnsville, Minn.*

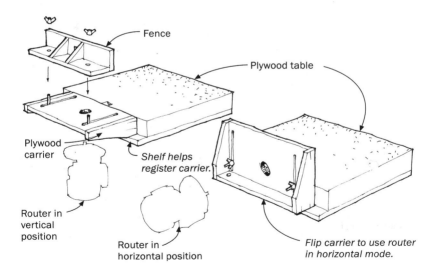

Fence

Plywood table

Plywood carrier

Shelf helps register carrier.

Router in vertical position

Router in horizontal position

Flip carrier to use router in horizontal mode.

Hinged Router Table

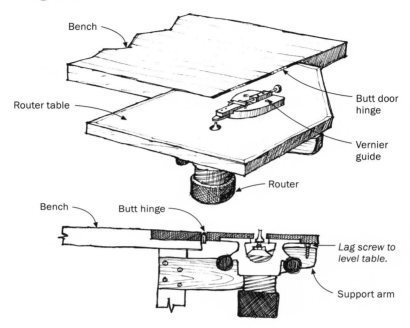

I SUSPECT THAT MANY OF US use our routers upside down, like a shaper, more than we do as a portable tool. I certainly do. But I don't like the flimsy metal stands sold for this use. They are too small and, used on top of the bench, are too high to be comfortable.

Here's a router table I built a couple of years ago that solves these problems.

The table is solid and set at a comfortable height. Because the tabletop hinges over, I don't have to squat down to remove the router, change cutters or adjust cutter height. I usually bolt, screw or clamp appropriate guides to the table for straight routing. For irregular contours I use a vernier-controlled guide as shown in the sketch. The vernier adjustment allows me to make two passes, removing most of the wood on the first pass and cleaning up the last $\frac{1}{16}$ in. on a final cut. I make the rub block on the guide from hardboard. Any unusual problem can usually be solved simply by making a new, specially shaped, hardboard rub block.

—JOHN W. GREENWOOD, *Dublin, Calif.*

Multipurpose Knockdown Router Table

I MADE MY ROUTER TABLE with a plywood top and a pair of sawhorses as legs. In order to allow easy knockdown, the tops of the sawhorses simply fit into dadoes beneath the plywood. This gives me a little more room in the shop when needed and frees the sawhorses when I want to use them for other things. The table has a spare router base permanently attached—the router can quickly slip out of this, put on its other bottom, and be ready to tackle other jobs. Best of all, I made the table the same height as my tablesaw, so it can double as an outfeed table, which is how the whole idea started.

—ED DEVLIN, *Rothsay, Minn.*

Space-Saving Router Table Mounts to Bench

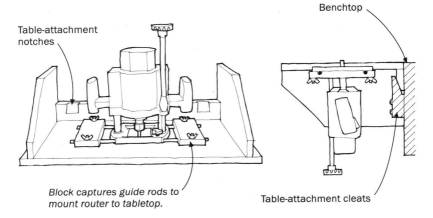

Table is shown upside down.

Benchtop

Table-attachment notches

Block captures guide rods to mount router to tabletop.

Table-attachment cleats

T HIS ROUTER TABLE is quick to set up and hangs on the wall when not in use. A plunge router attaches to the table's underside using the rods provided for the router's guide fence. Nothing need be removed from the router. Once the router is attached to the table, you can flip it over and slip the table onto wedge-shaped blocks bolted to the front of your workbench. The table is held securely by the blocks, and the total time for mounting or dismounting is minimal.

—D. A. KENNEDY, *Rugby, England*

Adjustable Router-Table Insert

W HEN I INSTALLED THE INSERT in my router table, I didn't
bother to rabbet the cutout hole to support the insert. Instead,
I attached spacer blocks and two lengths of angle iron (mine came
from an old bed frame) to the bottom of the router table. The edges of
the angle irons protruded into the cutout about an inch. I drilled a
pair of holes in each iron and inserted a carriage bolt in each hole, as
shown in the sketch. The four round-head bolts stick up into the
cutout space to support the plastic router insert at all four corners. By
adjusting the height of the four carriage bolts, the height of the insert
can be set to match the tabletop perfectly.

—MIKE HOLZHAUER, *Weare, N.H.*

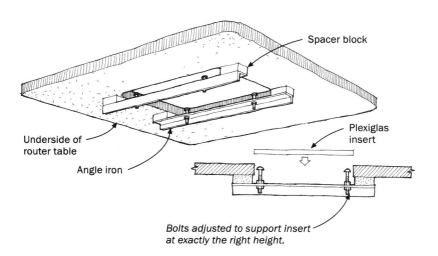

Spacer block

Underside of
router table

Angle iron

Plexiglas
insert

Bolts adjusted to support insert
at exactly the right height.

Router-Table Toggle Switch

T O AVOID GROPING AROUND UNDER THE TABLE to feel for the
router switch, I installed a switch-controlled receptacle so I can
turn the router on and off safely and conveniently. I mounted the
switch and receptacle on the front of the router table. You can use any
type of switch—just make sure it will carry the amperage. There are
plenty of other uses for the switch-controlled outlets (drills, sanders,
etc.); simply unplug the router when you don't want it to run.

   In addition, I made a 10-in.-sq. table insert for my router from
¼-in.-thick aluminum plate. I chose aluminum because it's easy to drill
out the mounting and spindle hole and, if polished, is almost friction-
free. The insert is held firmly in place with two countersunk, ¼-in.
flat-head machine screws into T-nuts in the tabletop. An accurately
inlaid insert won't float or vibrate.

—D. B. NEAGLEY, *Groveland, Calif.*

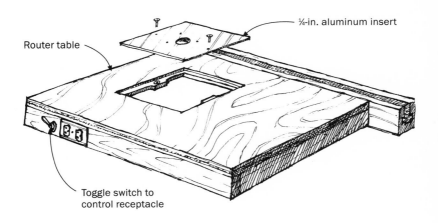

¼-in. aluminum insert

Router table

Toggle switch to
control receptacle

What's the Best Router for a Router Table?

F OR MY MONEY, the best choice for a router table is the fixed-base
Porter-Cable 7518 because the motor is easily extracted from the
base for bit changes. This tool has more vertical motor travel (more
than 3½ in.) than any router, whether plunge or fixed base. The 7518
(and 7519) has the biggest and most durable casting of any router,
and it's drilled and tapped for the largest screws (⅜-18). When this
casting is fastened to the underside of a router-table top, it acts as a
heavy mending plate and aids in flattening and strengthening the top.
This heavy-duty, soft-start, multi-speed tool can run for extended
periods (hours) on the toughest of materials (e.g., plastic, hardwood
and aluminum).

I would not use a plunge router in a router table. A plunge router is
primarily a multi-depth tool, and the router table is typically a single-
depth machine. Therefore, the rapid, multi-depth advantage of the
plunge router is lost. Also, plunge routers don't easily separate from
their bases, so the routers are usually mounted to a large piece of plastic and hung through a big hole in the router table to make bit changing easier. For precision joinery, a router-table top must be very flat. If
the top has a big hole in it, the integrity and equilibrium of the slab is
lost. Moreover, the interruptions of the mounting plate guarantee a
bumpy ride for the stock as it passes over the tabletop.

Plunge routers also use 4mm screws to mount the subbase.
Although adequate for this purpose, these screws are rather lightweight
for suspending a heavy router.

—PAT WARNER, *Escondido, Calif.,*
from a question by Ted Zogrotzki, Penn Valley, Pa.

Using a Plunge Router in a Router Table

M Y ADVICE FOR OUTFITTING a router table is to purchase a relatively inexpensive Sears router, bolt it on the table and forget about it. I would not use a large plunge router under a router table even though it has lots of power and handles those sturdy ½-in. shank bits. The problem with a plunge router is that it's hard to accurately adjust the depth of cut because you have to push upward against the stiff plunge spring.

—JIM ROME,
from a question by Jim Monroe, Beaver, Pa.

Quick Fix for Using Plunge Routers in a Router Table

I T HAS BEEN POINTED OUT that it is difficult to adjust a plunge router when it is mounted under a router table because you are fighting the plunge return springs. The simple solution to this problem is to remove the return springs. These springs are located in the base columns, and removing them is a five-minute job at most. You will then be able to raise and lower the router with ease.

—CHARLES D. HONL, *Burnsville, Minn.*

Scissors Jack Fence

AFTER YEARS OF ENDURING the inconvenience of removing and resetting numerous small bolts to adjust the fence on my router table, I made an adjustable fence that makes the whole process simple, rapid and accurate.

The fence is built around a used Toyota scissors jack that I found at an auto wrecking yard. First I spent a few minutes with a hacksaw to remove the portion of the jack that fits the underside of the car. Next I cut down the base to the width of the jack and bolted it to a ¾-in. plywood backboard. To make the fence, I attached a piece of straight, well-seasoned cherry to the top of the jack. With the careful use of shims, I set the face of the fence exactly perpendicular to the tabletop.

The fence is easy to adjust precisely. Once it's in position, I anchor it with small C-clamps on both ends. I suspect that these readily available scissors jacks could easily be adapted to a wide array of clamping, pressing and fine-adjustment problems.

—JOHN B. MOON, *Mount Vernon, Wash.*

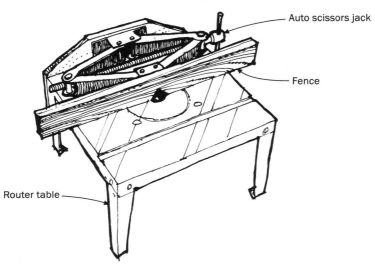

Auto scissors jack

Fence

Router table

Scissors Jack Router Lift

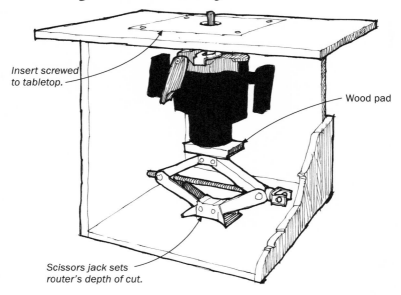

Insert screwed to tabletop.

Wood pad

Scissors jack sets router's depth of cut.

AFTER LOOKING THROUGH CATALOGS and saving my pennies, I finally located the perfect plunge router for my router table—or so I thought. After mounting it in the table, it became obvious that depth adjustments were difficult because I had to fight both the motor weight and the stiff plunge springs.

Using an automotive scissors jack is the solution that I've found. I place the jack below the router on a fixed shelf, mounting a small pad of wood on the top of the jack to protect the router. The only other change is to screw the drop-in insert to the table so that the jack won't push it out of the hole. Now I can set the depth of cut easily and accurately by turning the jackscrew with my fingers. When I have the right depth, I lock the router's plunge mechanism in that position and get on with routing.

—MARK G. CARIS, *Juneau, Alaska*

Crank Adjustment for Router Table

T HE MAKITA PLUNGE ROUTER I have installed in my router table
works beautifully. But adjusting the depth of the bit with the
adjustment knob was awkward and tedious. I solved this problem by
removing the preload springs from the router support tubes. Then I
fashioned a simple crank handle that screws to the existing knob. Now
I can adjust the router quickly to whatever depth I need.

—ROBERT T. COMBS, *Carpinteria, Calif.*

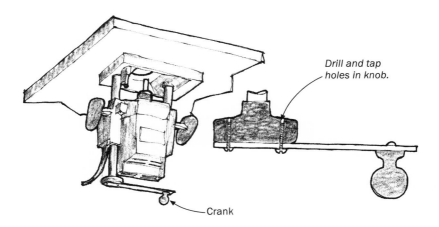

Drill and tap
holes in knob.

Crank

Router Table Uses Easy Toggle-Clamp Mount

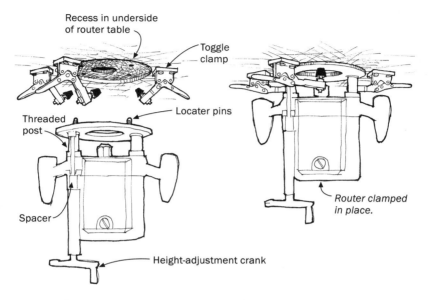

Recess in underside of router table

Toggle clamp

Locater pins

Threaded post

Spacer

Height-adjustment crank

Router clamped in place.

I F YOU'VE USED A ROUTER TABLE, you know firsthand the annoy-ances that go with mounting, dismounting and adjusting the router under the table. So when I redesigned my router table, I wanted a mounting method that was quick, secure and convenient, not only for installing router bits but also for adjusting their cutting depth. The approach I settled on uses three toggle clamps to hold the router under the table. The setup cost about $30.

To do this, first remove the router subbase and all the miscellaneous hardware attached to the base—wing nuts, stop turret and so on. If you are using a plunge router, buy and install a crank handle to the end of the threaded adjustment column. Recess the underside of the router table ¼ in. deep, and cut a 1½-in. hole in the center of the recess for the router bit.

Using the subbase mounting-screw locations, install locator pins in the base of the router, and drill mating guide holes in the router table. Make the pins by grinding the heads off machine screws. Screw three or four toggle clamps at convenient, equally spaced locations around the base of the router, and adjust their clamping action to hold the router firmly in place. Toggle clamps are available in several varieties and holding strengths, from 60 lb. to 1,000 lb. I'd advise some over-engineering here: for example, 200-lb. clamps with anti-vibration locks and horizontal handles.

Now I can dismount the router and have it on the tabletop ready for a bit change in about 10 seconds, and I don't have a mounting plate to work around. Mounting takes approximately 20 seconds.

—ARTHUR MARGOLESE, *Santa Rosa, Calif.*

Protecting the Router Bit

WHEN MY ROUTER TABLE ISN'T IN USE, I keep a 35mm film canister over the bit. It protects the cutting edges, keeps airborne dust from falling into the motor and reminds me to keep junk off the table.

—L. D. FREDRICK, *Aspen, Colo.*

Router-Table Mount
Allows Height Adjustment

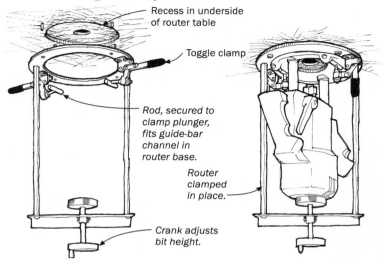

Recess in underside of router table

Toggle clamp

Rod, secured to clamp plunger, fits guide-bar channel in router base.

Router clamped in place.

Crank adjusts bit height.

T O ENABLE ME TO RAPIDLY INSERT and remove my router from the router table, I built the toggle-clamp fixture shown in the drawing. I removed the rubber cushions from the clamps and substituted short sections of steel rod, tapped through the middle like barrel nuts. The rods clamp into channels (for edge-guide rods) molded in my router's base.

The fixture also features an easy-to-use height-adjustment screw, which is simply a length of threaded rod fitted with a crank on the bottom and a pressure-dispersing disk on top. The screw eliminates the problem of having to overcome the combined force of the plunge router's weight and the spring pressure when making small height adjustments.

The all-metal fixture in the drawing does require moderate metal-working skills and access to some metalworking machinery. However, many of the components could be replaced by wooden counterparts.

—PHILIP BLUME, *Albuquerque, N.M.*

Combination Router-Table Bit Guard and Stops

I ADDED TWO 3-IN.-WIDE, 15-in.-long pieces of hardwood to the fence of my router table. Each piece is mitered on the end closest to the bit and attaches to the fence with round-head screws through a long slot. Now what have I got? First, I have a blade guard, which I can adjust to expose the minimum amount of cutting edge. Second, I have a built-in pair of stop blocks that can be quickly adjusted and locked without clamps.

—ROBERT SPALTER, *Lake Worth, Fla.*

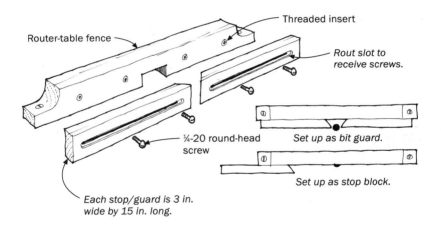

Router-table fence

Threaded insert

Rout slot to receive screws.

¼-20 round-head screw

Set up as bit guard.

Set up as stop block.

Each stop/guard is 3 in. wide by 15 in. long.

Pin-Router Attachment

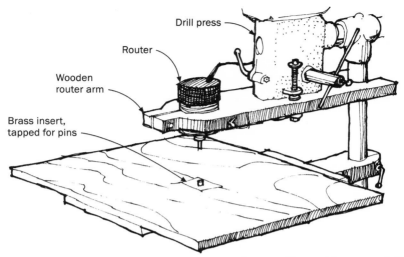

Drill press

Router

Wooden
router arm

Brass insert,
tapped for pins

B Y BOLTING A SIMPLE ROUTER ARM and an auxiliary table to my drill
press, I can convert it to a pin router. This lets me take advantage of
the drill press's quill movement to lower the router into the work.

Make the router arm from a 20-in. length of 2x6 lumber. Drill the
arm to fit your drill-press quill and feed stop, then notch the back of
the arm so it can slide up and down the post. On my drill press the
arm is held in place well enough by the drill-press feed-stop collar and
the feed stop. Other drill presses might require bolting the arm directly to the housing. In the end of the arm, cut a hole the same size as
your router. Then cut a slot in the arm and install a bolt to pinch the
router and lock it in place.

The table is a 20-in. by 30-in. panel of ¾-in. plywood covered with
plastic laminate and strengthened by a thick plywood spine on the
bottom. A tapped brass plate located in the center of the table accepts
different-diameter pins (I used standard router pins from Sears).

—ANDREW MAKAREVICH, *Villa Park, Ill.*

Pin-Router Adaptation for Radial-Arm Saw

YOU CAN EASILY CONVERT a radial-arm saw to a pin router. This tool will open up a whole new world of operations and make many familiar tasks—such as rabbeting for bookshelves or cutting mortises and slots—much easier.

To convert my Sears 10-in. saw, I merely duplicated on the lathe, in rock maple, the saw-motor attachment plug where it fits the motor-support arm. I laminated the ring assembly that holds the router from plywood. Then I glued and bolted together the laminated rings and the maple plug to form a single unit. Details of this fixture would vary to suit the saw/router combination. If the setup is combined with a machinist's dual-feed rotary table, very precise work is possible.

The router is normally used in the vertical position, but it can be rotated to any orientation (just like the saw) for special routing cuts.

—DONALD WIGFIELD, *Moneta, Va.*

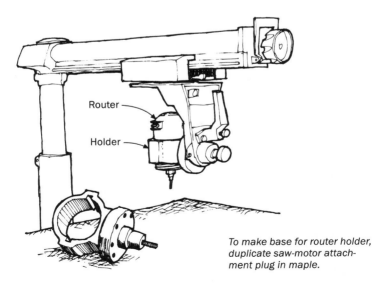

Router

Holder

To make base for router holder, duplicate saw-motor attachment plug in maple.

Router-Table Fence for Edging Discs

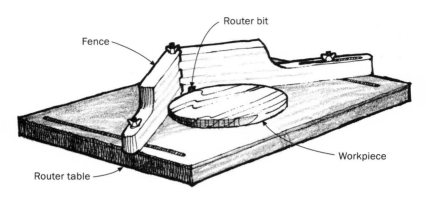

Router bit

Fence

Router table

Workpiece

I DEVELOPED THIS FENCE to shape the edges of round rings, such as clock bezels, on the router table. The fence can shape both outside and inside edges of circular blanks. When shaping the outside edge, some part of the profile must remain uncut to provide a bearing surface against the fence, or the disk would just keep spiraling smaller.

The fence is made by laminating 2-in.-wide, ½-in.-thick plywood strips into two arms that fit together in a finger joint that pivots on a ¼-in. bolt. Slots in both sides of the router-table top and in one arm of the fence allow adjustment for different-size circles and different-width rings.

The dimensions of the fence don't matter, but I've found that the angle between arms cannot be less than 90° for safety and should not be more than 135° or the workpiece rolls away from the bit. These extremes dictate the spread between the two slots in the router table and the length of the adjustment slot in the fence arm. With the setup shown, the work should be rotated counterclockwise, into the bit's rotation.

—ROBERT WARREN, *Camarillo, Calif.*

Holding Router Bits with Clay

W ITH MY ROUTER MOUNTED UPSIDE DOWN in a router table, I use a golf-ball size blob of children's clay or modeling compound to temporarily hold a router bit in place while I tighten the collet nut.

The material has just the right consistency to do this job and will not leave a residue on the router bit or the table. Pressed onto the router table and against the bit, the clay acts as a third hand to keep the bit from dropping too far into the collet.

This method gives me better control over making fine adjustments to the bit height than I get by dialing the router up and down. I store the material in a plastic bag to keep it from drying out.

—BOB KELLAND, *St. John's, Newfoundland*

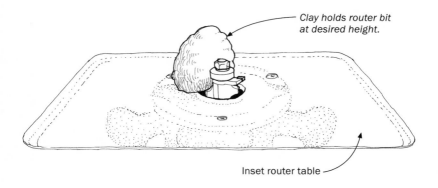

Clay holds router bit at desired height.

Inset router table

[Chapter 3]

BASES &
ALIGNMENT
FIXTURES

Two Asymmetrical Router Bases Solve Different Setup Problems

Roff's router base

Trivino's router base

Offset for cutting ⅝-in.-wide groove with ½-in.-dia. bit

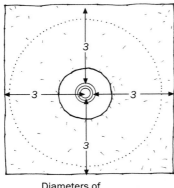

3
3 — 3
3

Diameters of commonly used bits

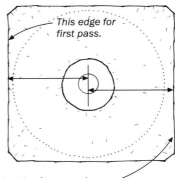

This edge for first pass.

This edge for second pass.

ROFF'S BASE: I used to get frustrated with the inordinate amount of time it took to set up my router for even the simplest cuts. The main problem was that the distance from the edge of the router base to the bit was always some weird dimension like 2¹⁹⁄₃₂ in. So recently, while making a new, custom router base out of Lexan, I got an idea.

I cut the rectangular base so that each of the four edges will be exactly 3 in. from the edge of one of my standard bits. For example, if I am using a ¼-in. bit, the edge marked ¼ in. will be exactly 3 in. from the edge of the bit. I also made one edge 3 in. from the center of the bit, which is frequently useful. In addition to writing the bit size on each edge, I color-coated the edges with permanent marking pens to help me remember which bit/edge I am using. To make the base, I cut the Lexan slightly oversize, and then, after mounting the router and making test cuts, I ran the base over a jointer to carefully trim each edge to the exact offset needed.

—DEREK ROFF, *Albuquerque, N.M.*

T RIVINO'S BASE: Recently, I needed to cut a large number of ⅜-in. grooves across several large pieces. Because I dislike using cutters larger than ½ in. in my small router and because I wanted to minimize the number of router-fence setups, I quickly designed and made the asymmetrical router baseplate shown in the drawing.

The theory is quite simple. Just vary the base's offset by the amount you want to enlarge the groove. In my case, I wanted to enlarge the ½-in. groove to ⅝ in. So I cut the base 3 in. from the center of the bit on one side and 3⅛ in. on the other, a difference of ⅛ in.

To use the fixture I set a fence parallel to the line of cut, made one pass with the first edge against the fence, and then made another pass with the second edge against the fence. One setup, two passes, one odd-size cut.

—ALLEN TRIVINO, *Rochester, N.Y.*

See-Through Router Base

I REMADE MY ROUTER SUBBASE out of ³⁄₁₆-in. Plexiglas, to increase visibility.

—JEROME CRAWFORD, *Durham, N.H.*

Purfling Router Guide

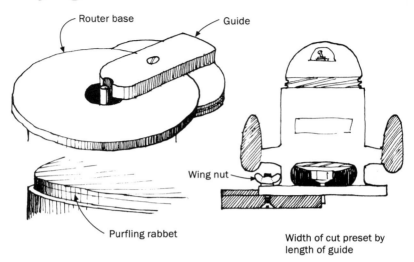

Router base

Guide

Wing nut

Purfling rabbet

Width of cut preset by
length of guide

I N STRINGED-INSTRUMENT CONSTRUCTION, the router is commonly used to cut a small shoulder around the perimeter of the instrument. The dado holds an ornamental inlay (purfling) used to cover the glue seam between top and side. The chore requires a precise cut with a router guide capable of following sharp curves. Though I've tinkered with various adjustable guides, I keep coming back to simple, wooden, preset guides.

The guide consists of a wooden finger glued to a crescent-shaped piece of plywood, which ensures proper positioning. A single bolt and wing nut provide fast but secure fastening.

For inlay work I have three guides, each made to cut a rabbet width corresponding to one, two, or three layers of veneer. Thus, for any given thickness of inlay, I just bolt on the right guide. No time is lost making practice cuts.

—GEORGE MUSTOE, *Bellingham, Wash.*

Two Shopmade Router Subbases

T HESE TWO ROUTER SUBBASES all but eliminate wavering cuts, plunge-cut kickouts and awkward balancing acts. Subbase No. 1 is made from ¼-in. Masonite or hardwood plywood. Mounted to the router in place of the regular base, the straight side of the subbase allows uniform fence pressure for rabbeting and positive control even after the bit has left the workpiece. I curved the other two sides to avoid confusion about which side of the triangle was indexed to the bit.

Subbase No. 2 sits straddlelike atop narrow-dimension stock. The lateral guides are adjustable to stock and groove locations. A simple system of slots with slides ensures rigidity and perpendicularity during use. The ⅜-in. carriage bolts and wing nuts make tightening easy and positive. The lateral guides eliminate plunge kickout and balance problems.

—BERNARD MAAS, *Cambridge Springs, Pa.*

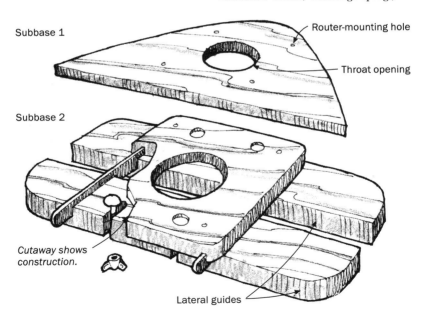

Subbase 1

Router-mounting hole

Throat opening

Subbase 2

Cutaway shows
construction.

Lateral guides

Edgebanding Thin-Skinned Plywood

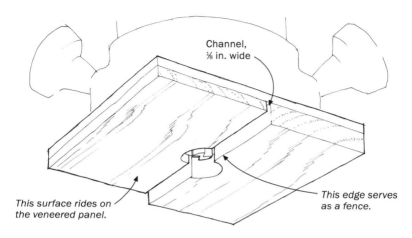

Channel,
⅛ in. wide

This surface rides on
the veneered panel.

This edge serves
as a fence.

E VERY WOODWORKER I KNOW has watched with dismay as veneered plywood has diminished in quality. These changes have
made it increasingly difficult to apply a solid edging and then trim it
flush to the panel without going through the plywood's thin face
veneer. This is because the face veneers have grown thinner and also
because of the indifferent quality of the core veneers. Part of the reason
for the decline of the core veneers is the availability of cheaper,
fiberboard-core veneered panels. Although fiberboard-core panels are
heavier, they are often preferred for their flatness and the excellent
finish they will take. To compete in price, the veneer-core product has
been adulterated. I encourage woodworkers to consider the fiberboard-
core panel for use wherever their design will permit it.

When edgebanding, I typically use a ⅛-in.-thick edgeband. For a
¾-in.-thick panel, I cut strips ⅞ in. to 1 in. wide. To draw this thin
edgeband tightly against the panel's edge, I always use clamping cauls

to evenly distribute clamp pressure. For a perfect, tight seam on larger projects, I apply one edgeband at a time, so I can observe the process closely.

With today's thinner veneers, be careful when trimming an edgeband flush with the panel's surface. I use a special router base, as shown in the drawing. A Bosch ½-in.-dia. hinge-mortising bit works best. With patience, you can adjust the bit to cut within thousandths of the veneered surface. To speed the process, I keep one router permanently set up for this operation.

I always move the router along the panel from right to left, so the bit's cutting sweep is inward toward the panel. This cutting direction preserves a crisp, unsplintered corner on the edging.

After routing, make a few quick strokes with a scraper blade to cut the edging flush with the surface. Then, blend the surface texture of the veneer and the edging with 220-grit sandpaper on a flat block. When leveling the banding along the end-grain edge of a panel, I rely more heavily on the sanding block. Beltsanding is out of the question, and on this particular operation, orbital sanders are neither faster nor do they leave a better surface.

To further protect the veneer (as well as save time and effort), I fanatically protect the factory-sanded surface. I will not lay the panels flat on a workbench top without first brushing it clean and scraping off all the glue lumps. And I do most of my sanding operations on a short-nap wool carpet.

—JOHN KRIEGHAUSER, *Chicago, Ill.,*
from a question by John W. Williams, Bellevue, Wash.

Router Jig for Flush Shelf Edging

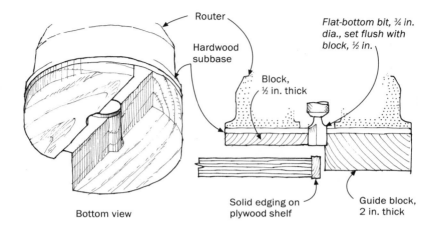

Router

Hardwood
subbase

Flat-bottom bit, ¾ in.
dia., set flush with
block, ½ in.

Block,
½ in. thick

Bottom view

Solid edging on
plywood shelf

Guide block,
2 in. thick

H ERE IS A ROUTER JIG for trimming edge moldings flush with a
flat surface. I have used this jig for trimming the edging on tables and countertops, but its most useful role is trimming solid-wood
edging on plywood to be used as adjustable shelves for bookcases.

The jig consists of two wood blocks screwed to a hardwood router
subbase. A ¾-in.-dia. flat-bottom router bit is set to cut flush with the
½-in.-thick block that rides on the surface of the plywood shelf. A
2-in.-thick block acts as a guide to run along the front of the shelf
edging. Run the router over each face of the shelf to trim the edging
flush with the plywood surface.

To save time when edging the shelves, I rip a ⅜-in.-wide, solid-wood strip that's about ⅛ in. thicker than the plywood. Then, I glue up a sandwich with the solid-wood strip between two of the shelves. You don't have to be very precise in aligning the edging and plywood because the extra ⅛-in. thickness will be trimmed off later. When the glue has cured, rip through the center of the edging stock on the tablesaw to separate the shelves, and then joint the face of the edging strips. To complete the shelves, attach the edging jig to the router and set the bit for a flush cut.

—LYNN NICKELSON, *Seattle, Wash.*

Storyboard for Routing Dadoes

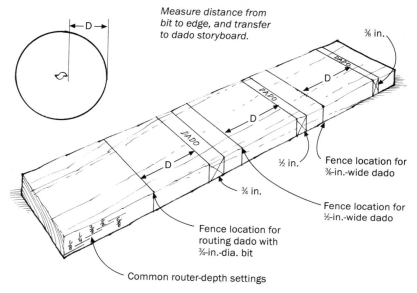

Measure distance from bit to edge, and transfer to dado storyboard.

Fence location for ⅜-in.-wide dado

Fence location for ½-in.-wide dado

Fence location for routing dado with ¾-in.-dia. bit

Common router-depth settings

H ERE'S A QUICK AND ACCURATE METHOD to determine where to clamp a guide fence when routing dadoes. First, measure the distance from the outside of your router base to the edge of the bits you commonly use for dadoes. Now, transfer each of these measurements to a ¾-in.-thick straight piece of wood, as shown in the sketch. To use the storyboard, simply align the dado lines with the desired dado location, and transfer the fence location mark to the workpiece. Also mark some commonly used depths on the edge of the storyboard to facilitate setting the depth of the bit.

—KEITH SCHUBERT, *Irvine, Calif.*

Storyboard for Routing Dadoes Revisited

I ADDED A COUPLE OF IMPROVEMENTS to Keith Schubert's dado-routing jig on the previous page. Rather than measuring and transferring the edge-to-bit distance from the router to the jig, I clamped a fence to each of the lines and routed a dado with the appropriate bit. This quick and accurate approach also makes it easy to see the location of the dado when using the jig.

An improvement for gauging bit depth (instead of making marks along the board's edge) is to bore holes of the appropriate depth in the end of the jig. Use your largest-diameter bit and a plunge router to drill the holes. The holes will ensure exactly the same depths every time, literally in seconds, without any measuring.

—GERARD R. MACK, *Badalasco, Italy*

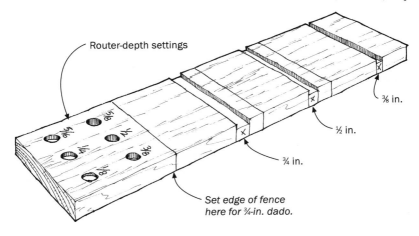

Router-depth settings

⅝ in.

½ in.

¾ in.

Set edge of fence here for ¾-in. dado.

Router Base with Extension Wing

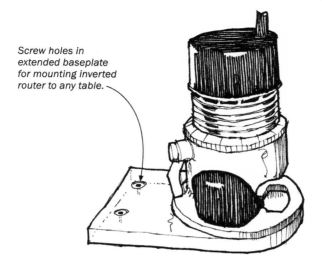

Screw holes in extended baseplate for mounting inverted router to any table.

I HAVE ONLY ONE ROUTER, and I wanted to use it as both a table-mounted and handheld tool. However, conventional router tables were too bulky, and frequently mounting and removing the router was too cumbersome. So I created a router base, as shown, with a wing that extends 3½ in. past the tool's base.

I made this wing from ½-in.-thick, clear-plastic Lexan, and screwed the wing to the router as a substitute for the manufacturer's stock baseplate. With the wing on the router, I can create an instant router table by running drywall screws through holes in the extension wing to fasten the inverted router to any suitable surface, such as a bench, windowsill, dock edge, toolbox or sawhorse.

As an added bonus, when I want to use the router as a handheld tool, the extension wing makes it easier to follow guides and keep the router level on narrow work and end cuts.

—GORDON ELLIOTT, *Friday Harbor, Wash.*

Wedge Quick-Clamp

O N MANY OF MY PROJECTS, I round over the front edges of large numbers of identical pieces of wood, such as shelves. Often the router-bit bearing extends below the bottom edge of the workpiece.

With a simple wedge–clamp system I can quickly secure a workpiece. The setup allows clearance for the router-bit bearing, and the thinner end blocks on each side of the workpiece allow clearance for the router base. I tap a wedge into place between the end block and an angled wedge block to hold the workpiece in place.

—JEAN V. RENSEL, *Sanborn, N.Y.*

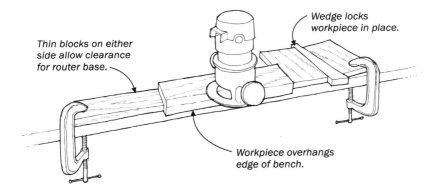

Wedge locks
workpiece in place.

Thin blocks on either
side allow clearance
for router base.

Workpiece overhangs
edge of bench.

Eccentric Router Base

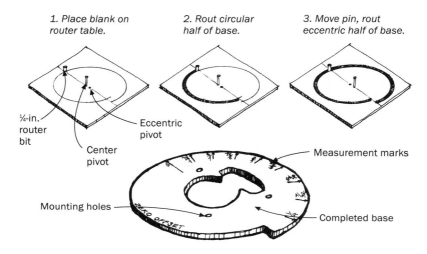

1. Place blank on router table.

2. Rout circular half of base.

3. Move pin, rout eccentric half of base.

¼-in. router bit

Eccentric pivot

Center pivot

Measurement marks

Mounting holes

ZERO OFFSET

Completed base

T HIS ROUTER SUBBASE allows me to rout an in–between size groove (for various stock thicknesses) without moving the guide fence or changing the setup. Because the subbase is eccentric to the router bit, you can change the diameter of the base simply by changing the point of the base that rides against the guide fence.

To make the base, choose plywood, plastic or a four-ply stack of plastic laminate for the material. You can cut the eccentric shape on a bandsaw or jigsaw, but for a smoother, more accurate base use a router table to machine the base. First drill a ⅟₁₆-in. pivot hole at the center of the blank for the base and another ⅟₁₆-in. pivot hole offset from the center. The offset determines the eccentricity of the base. I used an offset of ⅛ in., which allows me to cut grooves of up to ½ in. with a ¼-in. bit. On a line through these holes, drill a ¼-in. hole at a radius slightly larger than the radius of your router base. Before proceeding, it's a good idea to locate and drill the mounting holes in the subbase.

To cut the circumference of the base, mount the blank on the router table with the ¼-in. hole over a ¼-in. router bit. Drill 1/16-in. holes into the router table through both the center pivot and offset pivot. Put a pin in the center hole, turn on the router and rotate the subbase 180°. Return the blank to its starting position, put the pin in the offset hole and rotate the base 180° in the other direction. You will have to finish the "step" area with a file. Before routing out the center of the subbase, you should pivot the base on the center hole and scribe measurement lines on the base for every 1/32 in. of diameter change. Use a fine-tip waterproof pen.

To use the base to cut a 5/16-in. groove, for example, clamp a guide fence in place on the work and rout a ¼-in. groove. Keep the zero-offset part of the subbase against the fence. Now rotate the base until the 1/16-in. scribe line touches the fence. Keep the 1/16-in. mark touching the fence and make another pass, taking care not to twist the router. The result is a 5/16-in. groove.

—MIKE RAMEY, *Seattle, Wash.*

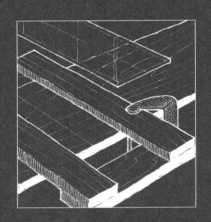

$[$ *Chapter 4* $]$

ROUTING
DADOES

Routing Dado Joints

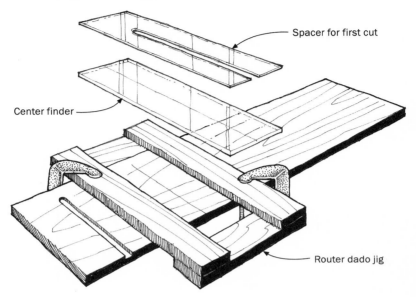

Spacer for first cut

Center finder

Router dado jig

IN THE HIGH-SCHOOL FURNITURE-MAKING CLASS I teach, we use a router and a parallel guide, like the one shown in the sketch, to cut most of our dado joints. Even though the guide alone helps reduce errors, we use two simple plastic fixtures to increase accuracy and reduce the number of mistakes made by new woodworkers.

The first fixture is a clear-plastic position finder, which we use to locate the guide quickly and accurately on the workpiece. To make one, cut the plastic the same width as your router base and as long as the guide. Then, scribe a centerline the length of the finder. To use it, first lay out the centerlines of the dadoes on your workpiece. Place the position finder in the guide, move the guide so the scribe line is positioned over the layout line and then clamp the guide in place.

The majority of our dado cuts are ¾ in. wide and ⅜ in. deep, which is too heavy a cut to make in one pass. Rather than reset the routing depth over and over for each cut, we use the second fixture, a ³⁄₁₆-in.- thick piece of plastic, as a spacer for the first cut. Like the finder above, cut the spacer the same width as the router base and the same length as the guide. Cut a 1-in. slot down the middle of the spacer to within a couple of inches of one end. To use, put the spacer between the guide fences, set the router for the full ⅜-in. depth of cut and make the first pass. Remove the spacer and make a second pass to the final depth.

—J. K. BLASIUS, *Bowling Green, Ohio*

Layout Procedure for Routing Dadoes

HERE'S MY PET METHOD for routing dadoes in plywood. First, locate and mark out the dado on the workpiece and score the veneer with a sharp knife. Set a compass to the distance from the edge of your router base to the bit. For example, if your router base is 6 in. across and you're using a ¾-in. bit, set the compass to 2⅝ in. With the compass point on one edge of the dado, swing two arcs—one at each end of the dado. Now clamp a straightedge tangent to the arcs to serve as a fence, and you're ready to rout.

—CHUCK ANDERSON, *Porterville, Calif.*

T-Square Router Guide

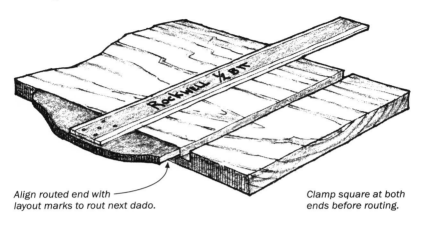

Align routed end with
layout marks to rout next dado.

Clamp square at both
ends before routing.

A COUPLE OF YEARS BACK, I grabbed an old drafting T-square for a woodworking student to use as a guide for routing a dado. When he approached the end of the cut, he stopped and told me that if he continued to the edge of the board, he would rout through the head of the square. Since I had a few spares around, I told him to go ahead. When he was finished, we were surprised to find that, by routing off the tip of the head, we had produced a very useful dado guide. The head of the square, now perfectly sized, could be used to align subsequent cuts with the same router and bit.

Now we have eight T-squares with lopped-off heads, each clearly marked as to the router and bit they go with. Four go with different size dadoes (¼ in., ⅜ in., ½ in. and ¾ in.) on a Sears router; the other four go with a Rockwell router.

The T-squares are handy for other operations as well. We use them with a ½-in. carbide bit in the router to "saw" wide or long boards to length if the operation is awkward on the tablesaw. Nothing could be squarer.

—JEFF SHERMAN, *Finn Rock, Ore.*

Dadoing Guide

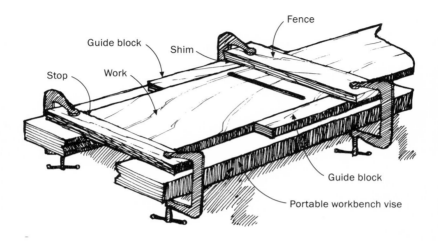

THE SKETCH SHOWS A QUICK SETUP I use for repeated dadoing operations with my router and portable workbench/vise. It's so simple, yet it's more accurate and quicker to use than the fence-clamped-to-the-board approach.

Make the parts from stock the same thickness as the boards you're dadoing. Clamp the fence atop two guide blocks to form a bridge over the work as shown. Shim the fence off the two guides with cardboard or veneer. This should leave enough clearance so the stock will slide in under the fence easily. Now, push the workpiece in under the bridge, snug against the stop. Clamp the workpiece to the workbench somewhere behind the fence. Set the router to proper depth and go to town. The blocks not only guide the workpiece, they also support the router base near the edge of the board.

—JOSH MARKEL, *Philadelphia, Pa.*

Easily Aligned Jig
for Routing Shelf Dadoes

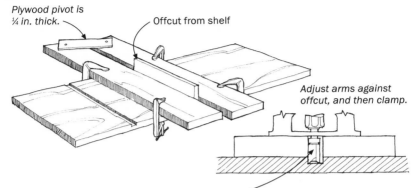

Plywood pivot is
¼ in. thick.

Offcut from shelf

Adjust arms against
offcut, and then clamp.

Remove offcut, and rout dado with
⅜-in. bearing-guided (patternmaking) bit.

RECENTLY, I HAD TO ROUT lots of dadoes in cabinet sides for
¾-in. plywood shelving. I came up with a method built around
a ⅜-in. flush-trimming router bit (with the bearing located above the
bit) and a simple jig made from two pieces of 1-in.-thick plywood
about 6 in. wide. The two pieces of plywood are joined at one end by
a small piece of ¼-in. plywood that pivots.

To use the fixture, clamp one side to the cabinet side along the
index line you have drawn for the shelf location. Position an offcut of
the same material you will be using for the shelf between the two
parts of the jig. Swing the second fence toward the first fence so that
it sandwiches the offcut, and clamp it in place. Now remove the offcut, and rout the dado, running the bit's bearing against the sides of
the jig's arms.

This system is more accurate than any other method I've used. It
even adjusts for minor variations in sheet thickness.

—ROBERT R. KNIGHTS, *Woombye, Australia*

Guide for Routing Dadoes

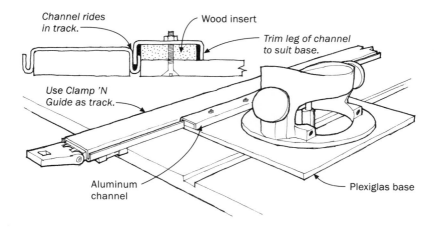

Channel rides in track.

Wood insert

Trim leg of channel to suit base.

Use Clamp 'N Guide as track.

Aluminum channel

Plexiglas base

AFTER LOOKING FOR AN EASY-TO-BUILD JIG to hold my router against a Clamp 'N Tool Guide (Griset Industries, Inc., P.O. Box 10114, Santa Ana, CA 92711; 800-662-2892), I suddenly came up with this idea that was the answer to my router-guiding problem.

First, I went out to the shop and gathered two items—an aluminum U-shaped channel, which fit the Clamp 'N Tool Guide quite well, and a leftover piece of Plexiglas. I cut off a 14-in. length of the channel and trimmed one leg, as shown. Then I milled a piece of oak to fit between the plastic and the channel. I assembled the parts temporarily with double-faced tape to keep everything in registration. Then I added three flat-head screws to hold things together permanently. In just a couple of hours, I was ready to cut my first dado.

Later, I realized that this idea would work equally well for a circular saw, substituting ¼-in.-thick Masonite for the Plexiglas base.

—JACK ZABEL, *Cedar Falls, Iowa*

Carcase-Dadoing Jig

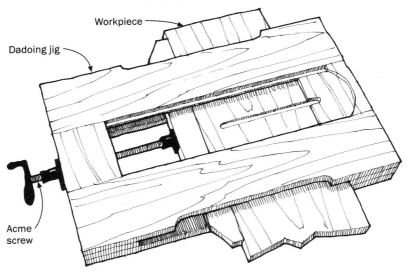

Workpiece

Dadoing jig

Acme
screw

THE MAIN ADVANTAGE to my homemade carcase-dadoing jig is the use of an Acme screw to lock the jig into position. Acme screws are often used in constructing book, cheese or juice presses and are available through many tool catalogs. I installed the screw as shown to make the positioning and clamping of the jig quick and accurate—certainly better than using C-clamps.

—CHARLES LEIK, *Great Falls, Va.*

Compensating for Inconsistent Plywood Thickness in Carcase Construction

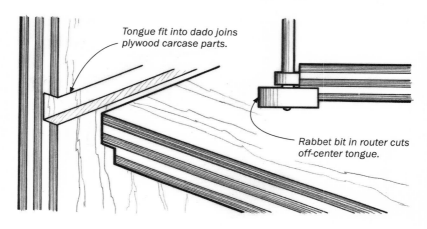

Tongue fit into dado joins plywood carcase parts.

Rabbet bit in router cuts off-center tongue.

I T'S ONE OF WOODWORKING'S BUGABOOS that materials said to be one dimension are often another. As many of you have discovered, ¾-in. plywood sheet-goods are usually less than ¾ in. thick. Many times, this is because they are imported and manufactured in metric sizes: 6mm, 12mm and 18mm. If your plywood is consistently ²³⁄₃₂ in. thick (18mm), you can purchase a special undersized dado bit for your router from Woodhaven (5323 W. Kimberly Rd., Davenport, IA 52806; 800-344-6657). However, in my experience, even a single sheet of higher-quality cabinet plywood can vary in thickness—a ¾-in. sheet can measure anywhere from about ⁴⁷⁄₆₄ in. to ²³⁄₃₂ in. or less. That is why few cabinetmakers I know will try to cut a dado to fit plywood's exact thickness. Usually the result is carcase joints that fit too loosely or too tightly.

One solution to perfect plywood carcase joints is to cut accurately sized tongues or rabbets on the end of plywood shelves or carcase parts and fit them into dadoes in the adjoining parts. Cutting a centered tongue has the advantage that both edges of the dado will be covered up when the joint is assembled, in case the dado cut is a little ragged. However, unless you have a special tongue-cutting bit for your shaper or router table, you'll have to cut the tongue in two passes. I prefer to shape a rabbet on the plywood edge instead, as shown in the drawing, like a sort of off-centered tongue. You can shape this tongue using a regular rabbet bit, top-piloted by a ball bearing slipped down over the bit's ¼-in. shank. The pilot bearing runs against the edge of the plywood (as shown). The length of the tongue can be adjusted by changing pilot bearings.

To adjust the fit, you can fine-tune the thickness of the tongue by varying the router bit's depth of cut. I usually make a test dado in scrap plywood first—cut with either a ½-in.-dia. straight router bit (for ¾-in. ply) or with a dado blade on the tablesaw. Then I make a test tongue in scrap to try the fit and adjust the cut until its thickness is just right. With this method, you'll get snug joints regardless of thickness variations in the plywood.

—SANDOR NAGYSZALANCZY,
from a question by Walter L. Flanigan, Pensacola, Fla.

[83]

Cutting Dadoes Safely

THE WORST ACCIDENT I ever saw in a woodshop involved someone hand-feeding plywood across a dado blade on a tablesaw. I'll spare you the gory details—suffice it to say that this is indeed a potentially dangerous operation. Because a dado blade has so much surface area immersed in the cut at any one time, it exerts a tremendous amount of force against the wood. Should the stock shift even slightly as it's being cut, the possibility of the dado blade violently grabbing and throwing the panel off the saw table is very real.

These days, I do not use dado blades to cut grooves in plywood. Instead, I set up a router with a grooving bit (router-bit manufacturers now offer cutters sized to nearly any thickness of plywood), and use the tool in conjunction with a simple shopmade cutting guide. (Saw Trax, a commercially made guide for this purpose, is available from Aardvark Tool Co., 2605 W. Alabama Road, #202, Acworth, GA 30101; 404-427-2414.)

There are a number of advantages of this method over dadoing. First, it is much safer. There is no chance of the router throwing the panel anywhere, and the cutting business of the router is well out of the way under the baseplate. Second, it does a better job. Unless the dado blades are extremely sharp and the tablesaw's arbor is free of wobble, tearout along the edge of the groove is inevitable. In contrast, the physics involved when making this cut with a router bit (high running speed and cutting-angle geometry) generally ensures a tear-free cut. And unlike the cut produced by a dado blade, a routed groove features a perfectly flat bottom—an important consideration if the joint is to show.

—JIM TOLPIN, *Port Townsend, Wash.,*
from a question by Alan Hayes, Chattanooga, Tenn.

Enlarging Routed Dadoes

I RECENTLY HAD TO ROUT a series of dadoes slightly wider than the router bit into some large panels. To accomplish this, I took advantage of my slightly eccentric router base. In relation to the collet, most router bases are less than perfectly centered.

Through trial and error, using pieces of scrap, I determined the high spot (the one farthest from the collet) and the low spot (the one nearest to the collet) on the base. I marked these locations with masking tape. I also marked several intermediate locations between high and low. With a fence clamped in place, I made a single pass, keeping the low spot against the fence. Then I rotated the router base, placing the high spot against the fence, and made a second pass to enlarge the original dado slightly. The second pass added about 1⁄32 in. of width to the dado—just the right amount for my application. If your router base happens to be concentric, you can accomplish the same effect by adding layers of tape as shims on the outside edge.

—SCOTT BOWEN, *Salt Lake City, Utah*

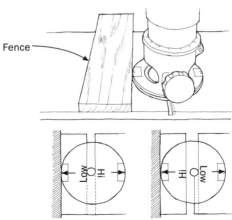

Find low spot and high spot on router base. Make first rout with low side against fence.

To enlarge dado, rout second pass with high side against fence.

Variable-Width Dado Fixture

Clamp fence to workpiece.

Run both edges of fixture against fence to cut wider groove.

THIS VARIABLE DADO FIXTURE will allow fine adjustment of the dado width from bit diameter to double-the-bit diameter. The fixture works on the principle that one edge of the router base is farther from the bit than the other. To use, clamp a fence in place on the workpiece and make one pass with the wide side of the fixture against the fence. Turn the router around (narrow side to the fence) and make a second pass.

To make the fixture, cut a 9-in. square from ¾-in. hardwood plywood, and rout a ½-in.-deep recess in the center to receive the router base. Rip one edge off the fixture and reattach it with two cleats, as shown. Slot one cleat to allow adjustment. The other cleat is fixed, and the adjustable edge is pinned to it so that the edge can pivot. You will have to trim the corner of the base outside the pivot point so that the adjustable edge won't bind. After the fixture is attached to the router, check to be sure that the distance from the bit to the adjustable edge is slightly (1⁄16 in.) less than the distance to the fixed edge. If it isn't, saw a little off. Otherwise, slight adjustments over bit size are impossible.

—JERE CARY, *Edmonds, Wash.*

Flip-Up Router Fence

W HEN ROUTING GROOVES, some people draw a line on the work where the groove will be, then calculate where to clamp the fence. Others draw the line where the fence will be, instead of marking the location of the groove. Both methods have obvious drawbacks.

But if you make a router fence that has a hinged extension, you can mark the center of the actual groove on the work, line up the extension with the mark, then flip it out of the way to rout the groove. Make the fence out of a straight, flat 1x4. Now rip another board half the diameter of your router base (measure from the center of the bit to the edge of the base), and secure it to the fence with flat hinges. As shown in the drawing, offset the hinges so that they won't protrude when the extension board is swung up out of the way.

—JAMES F. DUPLER, *Jamestown, N.Y.*

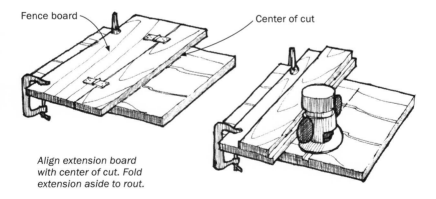

Fence board

Center of cut

Align extension board with center of cut. Fold extension aside to rout.

Jig for Cross-Grain Routing

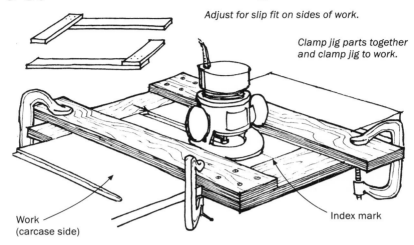

Adjust for slip fit on sides of work.

Clamp jig parts together and clamp jig to work.

Work
(carcase side)

Index mark

T HE CONCEPT IS SIMPLE, but this jig is indispensable for routing dadoes in carcase sides, especially when several dadoes are to be made in one board. Once the jig is clamped together you can slide it quickly into position for the next cut.

Make up two L-shaped pieces with 4-in. wide plywood strips. Cut the shorter pieces of the L 16 in. to 18 in. long (router base plus 8 in.) and the longer pieces 20 in. to 30 in. long (widest carcase plus 8 in.). Face-glue and screw the pieces together, taking care to maintain a 90° angle. To use, place one L on the front edge of the board to be routed and one on the back edge so that the two L's form a woven rectangle as shown. Adjust both directions to give a slip fit against the router base and against the sides of the board. Then clamp at the intersections of the two L's. Pencil in an index mark on both sides of the jig to simplify lining up for a cut. Clamp the jig to the board before routing the dado.

—ROGER DEATHERAGE, *Houston, Tex.*

Routing Tongues

I CUT THE TONGUES for tongue-and-groove joints with a router. There are faster methods, but the router's precision depth adjustment produces a fit that's unbeatable. First, set the router depth by trimming the edge of a scrap board. Flip the board over, trim the other side and test the resulting tongue in the groove (which has been previously cut). Make fine depth adjustments and continue to rout test tongues until the fit is perfect. To cut the tongue, first measure the distance from the router base to the bit. Then clamp a fence to the work this distance from the tongue. Gently tap the fence into perfect position with a mallet, checking the measurement with a steel ruler.

—JEFFREY COOPER, *Portsmouth, N.H.*

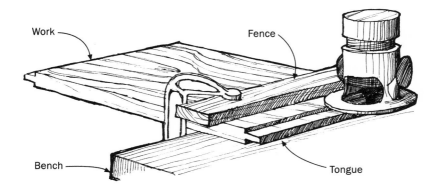

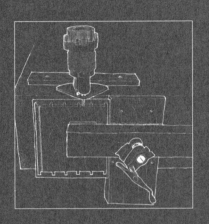

ROUTING
DOVETAILS

Homemade Router Dovetail Templates

Screw hardboard to router fixture, then
lay out and cut templates.

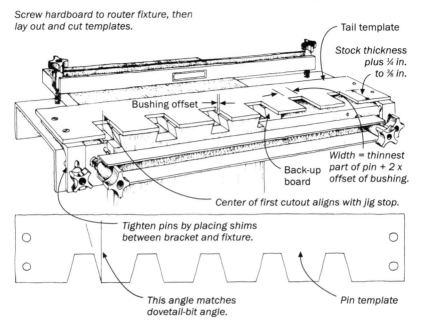

Tail template

Stock thickness
plus ¼ in.
to ⅜ in.

Bushing offset

Width = thinnest
part of pin + 2 x
offset of bushing.

Back-up
board

Center of first cutout aligns with jig stop.

Tighten pins by placing shims
between bracket and fixture.

This angle matches
dovetail-bit angle.

Pin template

B Y MAKING YOUR OWN TEMPLATES out of tempered hardboard, you
can rout through dovetails of any size and with any spacing using
the Sears-type dovetail jig. You will have to mill the pins and tails sep-
arately, with a straight and a dovetail router bit respectively.

I make my templates with slightly oversize fingers (see the drawing)
and then trim them down by trial and error until I get tight-fitting
joints. You'll have to take into account the outside diameter of the
router's guide bushing. Cut both the pins and the tails with the boards
mounted in the jig vertically. To prevent the exiting router bit from tear-
ing out the back of your stock, clamp a scrap in the jig horizontally.

—MICHAEL BOYTS, Crested Butte, Colo.

Varying the Spacing
of Template-Routed Dovetails

I VARY THE PIN/TAIL SPACING with my Rockwell dovetail jig (Sears-type) by inserting ⁷⁄₁₆-in.-dia. "coins" sliced from dowels between the fingers of the template. I insert a coin wherever I don't want a dovetail. The router follows the template in the usual way, but where the router's guide bushing encounters a coin, no tail will be cut.

To center pins and tails in the width of the stock, I cut dovetails in a 12-in.-wide scrap and keep this on hand as a gauge. When I lay out my joints, I butt the gauge and the stock end to end, centering the stock (it's usually narrower than the gauge) in the gauge's width. I mark where pins and tails are to be, and then measure the distance between one edge of the stock and the edge of the gauge. A scrap piece ripped to this measurement, crosscut in half and placed on both sides of the stock when it's mounted in the dovetailer, will automatically center the joint. If this centering leaves me with unattractive half-pins, I insert a coin and eliminate them.

—GEORGE R. KAHN, *Potsdam, N.Y.*

Routing Through Dovetails in ¾-in. Stock with a Leigh Jig

Y OU REPORTED THAT THE LEIGH DOVETAIL JIG will mill through dovetails in ¾-in.-thick stock only after you mill a rabbet in the pin board. But with a 14° carbide cutter (stock number DVO9-C, sold by M.T.D. Products Ltd., 97 Kent Ave., P.O. Box 1386, Kitchener, Ont. N2G 4J1), this jig can be made to dovetail ¾-in. stock without cutting the rabbet. This bit has a ¾-in. cutting depth instead of the ½-in. depth of standard bits. It must be used with a ⅝-in. guide bushing mounted in the router. I limit tearout when cutting the tails by first wasting most of the wood with a 5⁄16-in. or a ⅜-in. straight bit, followed by a clean-up cut with the dovetail bit.

—ANGELO CIFELLI, *East Hanover, N.J.*

Routing "Hand-Cut" Dovetail Pins

M Y VARIATION ON ROUTING DOVETAILS involves cutting the pins with a router equipped with a ¼-in. straight bit and a bushing that follows an acrylic template. This approach allows variable-sized pins that look hand-cut. The tails are later marked from the pins and chopped out by hand in the traditional way.

I mark the pins on the edge of the workpiece, and clamp the work to a fixture made of 1⅛-in. particleboard. For through dovetails, sandwich a piece of scrap between the work and the fixture to prevent tearout in the workpiece and damage to the fixture. For blind dovetails, clamp the work directly to the fixture. Slide the template into position over the workpiece to control the spacing between the pins.

I've cut several opening sizes on mine. They vary the pin spacing between ¾ in. and 2¼ in., in ⅛-in. increments, depending on the bushing. For accuracy, make the template's angled cuts on the tablesaw.

Clamp the template into place with two toggle clamps, as shown. Set the router to the desired depth, and remove the material between the first two pins. Loosen the clamps, and reposition the template by eye to the layout lines for the next cut. It takes less than five minutes to cut the pins on one edge of a typical drawer. When cutting half-blind dovetails, the router bit leaves rounded inside corners that must be cleaned up with a chisel.

To complete the joint, I mark the tails from the pins and cut to the lines with a bandsaw. I chop out the waste with a chisel.

—JIM HALE, *Saline, Mich.*

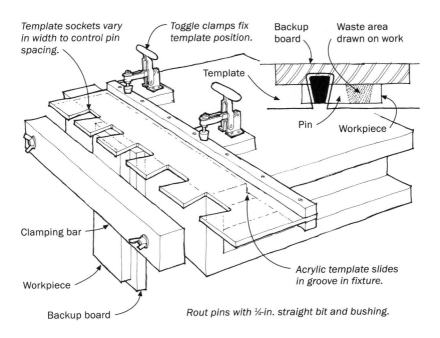

Template sockets vary in width to control pin spacing.

Toggle clamps fix template position.

Backup board

Waste area drawn on work

Template

Pin

Workpiece

Clamping bar

Workpiece

Backup board

Acrylic template slides in groove in fixture.

Rout pins with ¼-in. straight bit and bushing.

Removing Dovetail Waste with a Router

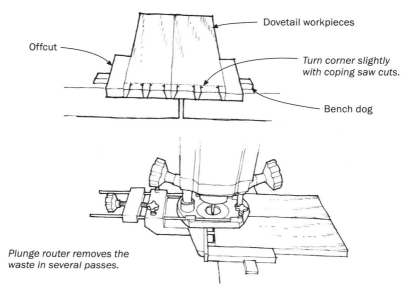

Dovetail workpieces

Offcut

Turn corner slightly
with coping saw cuts.

Bench dog

Plunge router removes the
waste in several passes.

USING A CHISEL TO CHOP out the waste between dovetail pins and tails is both tedious and time-consuming. So I speed up the operation by using a router fitted with a fence and a small-diameter bit. This technique works especially well with large dovetails.

To use this technique, lay out and cut the pins first. With a coping saw, turn the corner slightly at the bottom edge of the waste piece. This will allow the waste to drop out cleanly when routing. On the edge of the bench, sandwich two workpieces between two offcuts of the same thickness and clamp them all together with bench dogs. Orient the workpieces so that the widest part of the pin is up; otherwise, you'll cut off part of the pin as you plunge through with the router. Set up a small plunge router with a fence so that the bit cuts exactly on the line. Plunge through the waste starting as near to the dovetail sawcuts as you dare. Do this in as many steps as required, nibbling away a small amount at a time. To complete the joint, chop out the corners left by the router with a wide chisel, guiding the chisel on the flat areas removed by the router.

—RICHARD JONES, *Houston, Tex.*

Improved Dovetail Jig

To speed up routing of dovetail joints, replace the screw knobs on your template jig with fast-acting toggle clamps. Place springs under the hold-down bars, so they raise when the clamps are released.

—JON MATTHIAE, *St. Paul, Minn.*

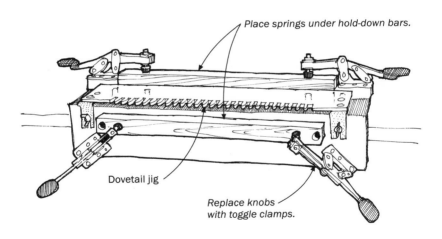

Place springs under hold-down bars.

Dovetail jig

Replace knobs with toggle clamps.

Dovetailing with a Laminate Trimmer

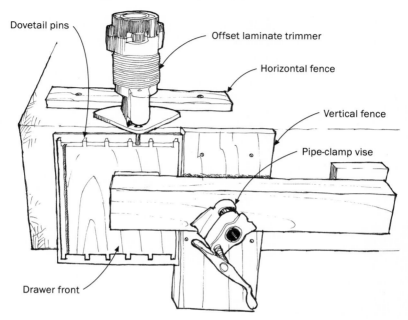

Dovetail pins

Offset laminate trimmer

Horizontal fence

Vertical fence

Pipe-clamp vise

Drawer front

T HE MOST TIME-CONSUMING PART of dovetailing drawers is the tedious tap-tap-tapping with mallet and chisel to cut the half-blind pins in the drawer fronts. So, when I was faced with making eight mahogany drawers with a ¼-in. overlay on the fronts, I decided to cut these pins with an offset laminate trimmer that I'd recently acquired. The method I devised takes advantage of the offset trimmer's unique features: It provides excellent visibility of the bit, is small and lightweight and has an offset center of gravity. The resulting pins are speedily and easily cut without looking as if they were mass-produced with a jig.

First, I laid out the tails on the drawer sides and then bandsawed them out. Because the backs were joined with simple through dovetails, I marked the pins from the tails and bandsawed them.

After marking the pin locations for the half-blind dovetails on the drawer fronts, I clamped one of the fronts to the side of my worktable using a special setup and pipe-clamp vise, as shown in the drawing. Two fences are key to the setup. The vertical fence is fastened to the side of the workbench and registers the drawer front to ensure that it's perfectly square with the top of the table. The horizontal fence is screwed to the tabletop and acts as a guide to run the base of the router against. This fence is set parallel with the edge of the table and just far enough away from the edge to leave the proper lip on the drawer front.

To cut the pins I chucked a ⁵⁄₁₆-in. straight router bit in the trimmer and adjusted the drawer front in the vise so that the depth of cut was right to the line representing the thickness of the side piece. I turned on the trimmer and carefully wasted the areas between the pins by routing right up to the scribed lines. When the routing was complete, very little trimming with a chisel was necessary to clean up the joint.

The offset trimmer is particularly well suited for this kind of work because its center of gravity is over the table, not over the bit. For safety's sake, be sure to use a face shield and goggles to keep the blizzard of little wood flakes out of your eyes.

—JOHN E. JANBAZ, *Amarillo, Tex.*

Trimming Dovetails

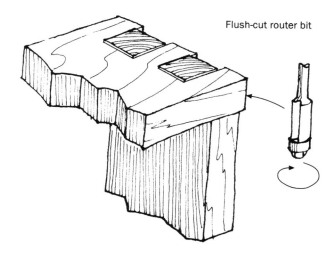

Flush-cut router bit

WITH THROUGH DOVETAILS it's accepted procedure to cut the joints a bit long and trim the ends flush after gluing. The fastest method I've found for trimming the slight overhang is to use a router equipped with a carbide-tipped, ball-bearing flush-trim bit. Start the cut at the very corner to prevent the bit from grabbing at the beginning. Always feed against the direction of the cutter rotation. After routing, a light planing or sanding will complete the job.

—DON HERMAN, *Brecksville, Ohio*

Jig for Routing Sliding Dovetails

WHEN I WAS INSPIRED to use sliding dovetails on a project, I designed this jig with a pivoting fence mounted on the router's enlarged baseplate. With the whole fixture attached to the router, it becomes portable. I can move the bit across the wood rather than having to move the wood across the bit. With long pieces, this can be a big advantage in a small shop.

To cut the dovetail slot, I remove the fence entirely and slide the baseplate against an auxiliary fence clamped to the workpiece. Then, I reattach the fence and adjust it to cut the correct size dovetail to fit the slot. I mark where the fence is set so I can repeat the setting.

—LARRY NAUMANN, *St. Louis, Mo.*

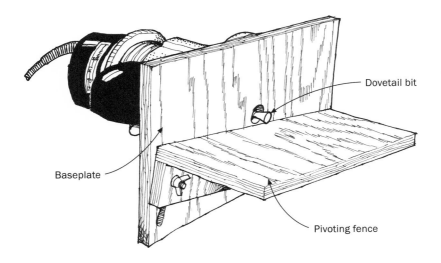

Dovetail bit

Baseplate

Pivoting fence

T-Guide for Cutting Sliding Dovetails

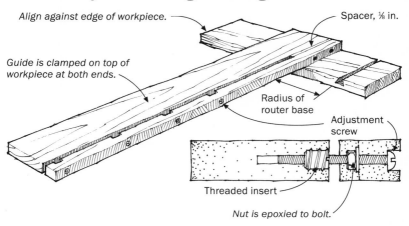

Align against edge of workpiece.

Spacer, ⅛ in.

Guide is clamped on top of workpiece at both ends.

Radius of router base

Adjustment screw

Threaded insert

Nut is epoxied to bolt.

T HIS T-GUIDE ADJUSTS so you can rout a sliding dovetail slot that is slightly wider at one end. The tapered slot allows easier insertion of the dovetail cleat but does not compromise the integrity of the joint. Construction of the guide is straightforward, as shown above. For the adjustment action, I installed ¼-in. machine bolts and threaded inserts every 6 in. along the arm. Nuts epoxied to the screw threads provide leverage for moving the arm in and out.

To rout a tapered dovetail, I clamp the guide to the panel at both ends. After making one pass with the router to cut a uniform-width dovetail slot, I turn the adjustment screws to move the flexible part of the guide arm out a bit—just a quarter turn or so at the far end is usually enough. Then I make another pass with the router to produce a slot that is slightly wider at one end. To complete the joint, I cut the dovetail on the cleat in the standard way using a router table.

—H. WESLEY PHILLIPS, *Greer, S.C.*

Sliding Dovetail Fixture

WHILE ATTEMPTING TO ROUT long sliding dovetails on the end of shelving joints, I found it impossible to keep the overwide and long shelves perpendicular to my router table. Here is a fixture I devised that, in effect, brings the table to the work. It's a platform with a slot in the middle and two perpendiculars for sandwiching the work. To rout the dovetail, I clamp the work in the jig flush with the top of the platform. Two fences, attached at the proper spacing, guide the router and ensure a consistent dovetail.

—VICTOR GAINES, *Glenside, Pa.*

Cut slot in table longer than work.

End of work in table slot

Jig for Sliding Dovetail Housings

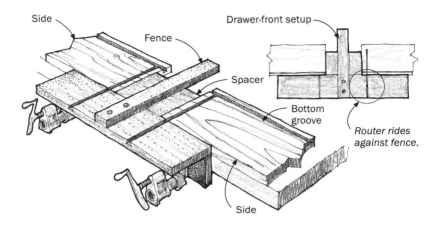

Side

Fence

Drawer-front setup

Spacer

Bottom groove

Router rides against fence.

Side

I USE A SIMPLE BUT EFFECTIVE JIG to cut housings for sliding dovetails in drawer construction. The jig consists of an L-shaped shelf, a fence to guide the router and a spacer board screwed to the fence from the bottom. The jig is clamped to the front of the workbench from underneath with pipe clamps and is carefully adjusted so the height of the shelf matches the thickness of the drawer stock.

The jig is designed so that housings are cut ½ in. from the end of the workpiece. If necessary, adjust the size of the spacer to locate the housing farther from the edge. The grooves for the drawer bottom are cut in the drawer front and sides before the jig is used.

To use the jig, butt two sides up to the stop as shown, with the grooves at the far side of the drawer stock. Move the router in from the front of the jig, and stop the cut at the groove. To cut the housings in the drawer front, place the front so it faces in the opposite direction, with the bottom groove in front. Rout through the groove, stopping the cut for the housing at the desired distance from the top edge (usually ½ in. or so). This way, the sliding dovetail is not exposed at the top edge of the drawer's front.

To rout the male dovetails, I use a tall fence on my router table with the router attached to the back of the fence and the bit running parallel to the table. I recommend cutting one side of the dovetail on all the pieces, then resetting the fence and cutting the other side with the same face against the table as before. The principle of always working relative to one face will ensure that all dovetails will be the same size.

—BARRIE GRAHAM, *Arundel, Que., Canada*

Jig for Routing Sliding Dovetails in Drawer Fronts

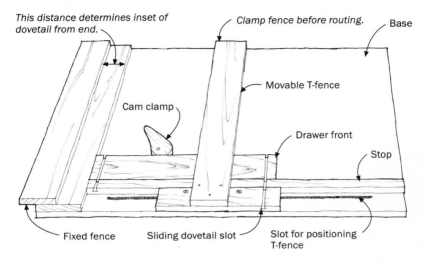

This distance determines inset of dovetail from end.

Clamp fence before routing.

Base

Movable T-fence

Cam clamp

Drawer front

Stop

Fixed fence

Sliding dovetail slot

Slot for positioning T-fence

I RECENTLY RECEIVED AN ORDER for drawers joined at the front with sliding dovetails. Because the drawers were of many different sizes, I needed to make a router jig that would accommodate drawer fronts of different lengths and widths. The jig I came up with consists of a base with a fixed fence on one edge and a movable T-fence on the other edge. The workpiece is aligned against a stop attached to the base at the front of the jig. The T-fence moves left and right to allow for various widths of drawer fronts, and it locks in place with bolts and wing nuts. I also clamp the T-fence front and back with C-clamps for extra rigidity. A cam clamp holds the work tightly against the stop.

To make through-sliding dovetails, clamp the workpiece in place, and rout both sides with the router. To make stopped-sliding dovetails, either make a stop or draw a stop line on the drawer front about ½ in. from the edge.

—ROBERT S. KUMMEROW, *Elmhurst, Ill.*

Sliding Dovetail Joint for Butcher-Block Table

S OME OLD BUTCHER TABLES were laminated up with 8-in.-long blocks locked together with double-sliding dovetails. To make this difficult joint, joint and plane the wood and be sure all pieces are straight. For the male part, remove most of the wood using a hand router or dado blade. Use a router table with a fence and cut A (shown here) in all the pieces. Then reset the fence for B, C and D. Be sure to have the same edge against the fence for each cut. For the female part, remove most of the wood with a straight cutter. Use the router table with the fence, as when making the male joint.

Perhaps a better and easier approach is to make all the joints female and then make a loose feather on the router table, using the same cutter. This wastes less wood and can be more decorative, especially if you use contrasting species.

—TAGE FRID, *from a question by George Selfridge, Mosier, Ore.*

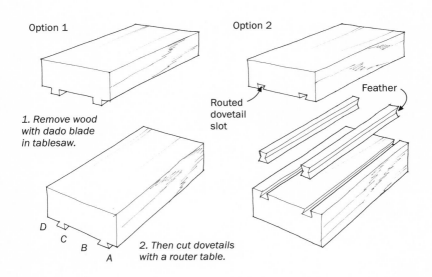

Option 1

1. Remove wood with dado blade in tablesaw.

2. Then cut dovetails with a router table.

D
C
B
A

Option 2

Routed dovetail slot

Feather

Sliding Dovetail Jig

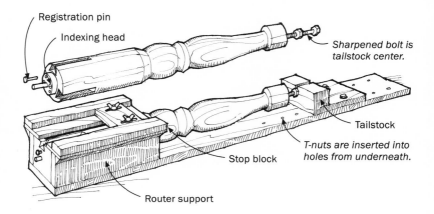

Registration pin

Indexing head

Sharpened bolt is
tailstock center.

Tailstock

T-nuts are inserted into
holes from underneath.

Stop block

Router support

I USE THIS JIG FOR ROUTING the sliding dovetail housings for the legs
of small pedestal tables and stands: It's fast to set up and very accurate. I made the jig's index head from a ½-in.-thick aluminum plate
bandsawn into a circle, but you can make it just as easily out of a thick
piece of hard maple. I tapped the center of the index head to receive a
short length of ½-in.-dia. aluminum rod, with one end protruding
slightly and pointed to act as a center. Three indexing holes are bored
through the head to correspond with the dovetail housings to be cut
in the pedestal. A registration pin pushed through the face of the
router support seats in one of these holes, positioning the pedestal for
routing.

I use a ¾-in. dovetail cutter in my router to cut the housings, and
install an adjustable stop block on the router support to keep the
housings the same length.

—ERIC SCHRAMM, *Los Gatos, Calif.*

Routing Dovetail Slots for Shaker Table Legs

T HE SHAKER PEDESTAL table is inexpensive to build and requires only six wooden parts and a handful of screws. The only construction
problem is cutting the sliding dovetail housings for the legs. The jig
shown solves this problem.

To use the jig, build up a hexagonal turning blank for the table's stem,
chuck it in the lathe and turn the lower 5 in. of the stem to size. Now
remove the blank from the lathe, mark out the centerlines for the dovetail cuts on three sides of the stem, and mount the jig on the workpiece.

The jig has two halves that mate with the hexagonal part of the
workpiece, thereby positioning the turned section under the router
guide slot.

A bench vise holds the setup. Start by hogging out all three dovetail
slots with a ⅜-in. straight bit. Use your router's guide bushing to guide
the cut. Next, clean out the slots with a dovetail bit. After the dovetail
slots have been cut, return the stem to the lathe to complete the turning.

—BERNIE MAAS, *Cambridge Springs, Pa.*

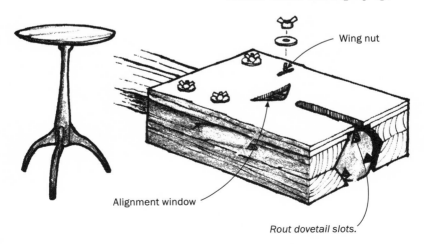

Wing nut

Alignment window

Rout dovetail slots.

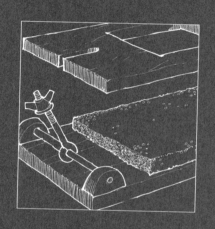

[*Chapter 6*]

ROUTING MORTISES & CAVITIES

Router-Mortising Jig

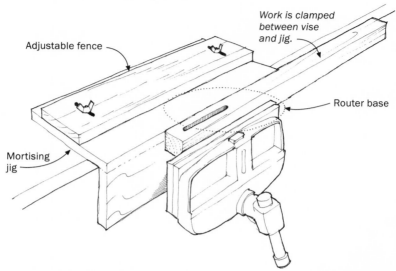

Work is clamped between vise and jig.

Adjustable fence

Router base

Mortising jig

WITH THIS SIMPLE JIG and a plunge router, you can rout mortises or panel grooves in any size leg or rail. The work is held between the jig and your bench vise, clamped flush with the surface of the jig, which provides a stable base for the router. Adjust the fence back or forth to orient the router cut to the workpiece. For longer pieces, make a longer jig, and clamp the workpiece at each end.

—ANTHONY GUIDICE, *St. Louis, Mo.*

Two-Position Router-Mortising Fixture

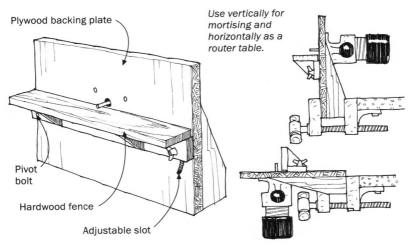

Plywood backing plate

Use vertically for mortising and horizontally as a router table.

Pivot bolt

Hardwood fence

Adjustable slot

THIS ROUTER MORTISING FIXTURE clamps in a bench vise and can be used vertically, like a mortising machine, or horizontally, like a router table. To locate the mortise, the fixture features a pivoting fence, which I believe is an easier and more consistent adjustment than pivoting the router.

To make the fixture, first mount the router to a plywood or particleboard backing plate; a sink cutout from a countertop is ideal. On the back of the plate, rout out a seat for the tool's base, leaving about ¼ in. of material, and mount it in the seat with machine screws countersunk in the top surface. The adjustable hardwood fence is attached to the backing plate with a pivot bolt on one end and a bolt and wing nut through a slot on the other end, as shown. This approach allows for very fine adjustments, because when you raise or lower the end of the fence, it moves only half as much under the bit.

Screw a cleat across the back underside of the plate so that you can hold the fixture in your vise horizontally, making a fine router table.

—STEVEN HJEMBOE, *St. Paul, Minn.*

Self-Made Mortising Template

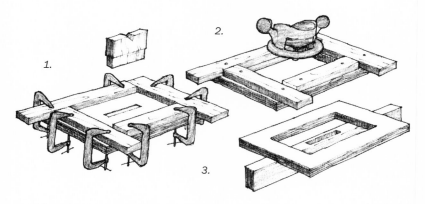

T HIS PROCEDURE FOR MAKING a router template is quite accurate. First, lay out the mortise dimensions on the template stock. Now, with the router and bit you intend to use, line up the bit with one wall of the mortise. Clamp a strip parallel to the mortise side so it butts against the router base, thus defining one side of the mortise. Repeat the process on the other three sides.

Now, as a test, rout a shallow mortise in the template stock. If the tenon does not fit, move and reclamp the guide boards. If the mortise is slightly oversized, you can add shims. Then cut another test mortise, a little deeper, and repeat until you have the fit you want. Next, screw the guide strips in position, countersink the screw heads and remove the clamps.

To finish the template, cut out the center of the blank and trim the edges flush with a router and a flush-cutting bit as shown in step 2, then remove the guide strips.

—PATRICK WARNER, *Escondido, Calif.*

Mortising Fixture

THE SIDES OF A CRADLE I built recently were made of slats mortised into the frame. The router-based mortising fixture I built for the project helped me cut all those little mortises quickly and easily.

The fixture has three simple pieces: a hardwood clamping lip, a birch-plywood router base and a Masonite hold-down. Bolt the 2x3 clamping lip under the workbench flush with the front edge. To permit deeper mortises, rout a ⅜-in. recess in the plywood base to fit the router. Mount the router in this recess using countersunk screws driven from the face.

To use, clamp the base to the clamping lip, making sure the bit is the right height above the workbench. Then clamp the hold-down in place. Stand behind the router and, sighting from above, pull the workpiece into the router. A router cut or pencil lines on the hold-down are needed to show the left and right boundaries of the cut. Feed the work from right to left. The router produces mortises with rounded ends, which can be squared up with a chisel. But it's easier to round the tenons with a rasp or sandpaper.

—G. R. LIVINGSTON, *New York, N.Y.*

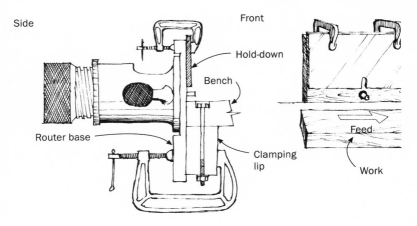

Side

Front

Hold-down

Bench

Router base

Clamping lip

Feed

Work

Improved Horizontal Mortiser

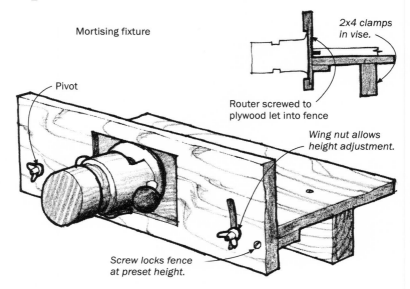

Mortising fixture

2x4 clamps
in vise.

Pivot

Router screwed to
plywood let into fence

Wing nut allows
height adjustment.

Screw locks fence
at preset height.

THIS HORIZONTAL MORTISING ROUTER jig is a more versatile adaptation of G.R. Livingston's jig shown on the previous page. The jig can be clamped in a vise but is fully portable and could be clamped to a sawhorse, for example.

The fence is adjustable by means of two bolts and wing nuts, which lets you center the mortise in stock of different thickness. The fence can be locked in preset positions (for mortising ¾-in. stock, for example) with a screw through the fence into the frame behind. My version of the jig is made from plastic-laminate-covered particleboard sold for shelving. I mounted the router on a piece of ¼-in. birch plywood recessed into the face of the fence.

—CHARLES W. MILBURN, *Weston, Ont., Canada*

Routing Deep Through Mortises

H ERE'S A SIMPLE BUT EFFECTIVE WAY to cut deep through mortises. First rout the mortise halfway through from the face edge of the stock. Then drill out the majority of the waste through the member. Mount a ball-bearing flush-trim bit in the router and clean up the mortise from the back edge of the stock. Be sure the trimmer bit's bearing is deep enough to ride on the dressed portion of the mortise. Of course, you will have to square out the corners by hand.

—PATRICK WARNER, *Escondido, Calif.*

Rout mortise to depth of bit.

Drill out waste.

Complete mortise from other side with flush-trim bit.

Pivoting Router-Mortising Fixture

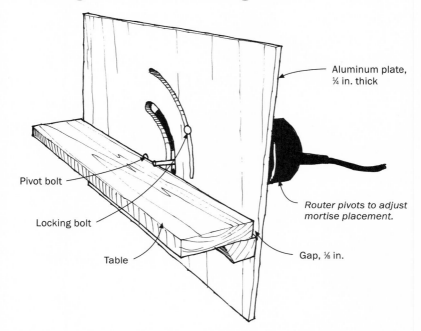

Aluminum plate,
¼ in. thick

*Router pivots to adjust
mortise placement.*

Pivot bolt

Locking bolt

Table

Gap, ⅛ in.

ECAUSE I NEEDED TO CUT more than 400 mortises in a short
period of time, I built this pivoting router fixture. With it, I can
cut two mortises in about one minute, including the layout time, so
the four hours I spent building the jig were quickly repaid.

The router is attached to an aluminum plate with a single bolt so it
will pivot to adjust for the position of the mortise in the stock. The plate
has two concentric slots centered on the pivot bolt: one for the mortising
bit and one for a locking bolt and wing nut. A cleat to support the table
is screwed to the plate, and a hardwood table is glued and screwed to the
cleat with a ⅛-in. gap left between the table and plate for chip and dust

clearance. My aluminum plate is ¼ in. by 12 in. by 20 in. I recommend 6061 aluminum with a hardness of at least T3. You can mill the curved slots in the plate by building a special pivoting fixture and using a milling cutter in the drill press. Or, if you're patient and careful, you can rout the slots with a router and double-flute carbide bits with a trammel or circle-cutting fixture. Take several light cuts. After the plate is completed, install the fence and attach your router.

To use the mortising jig, bolt or clamp it to the edge of a stout table or workbench. Adjust the router for mortise placement and depth of cut. Then, start the router and push the stock from left to right past the bit. Plunge the stock onto the bit for stopped mortises. Use stop blocks for repetitive cuts or draw layout lines on your stock to show you where to start and stop your mortise in relation to the bit's slot. Don't try to mortise pieces that are too narrow or are shorter than about 12 in. In addition, use the same caution you would with any router-table operation.

—JAMES E. GIER, *Pine, Ariz.*

Router-Height Adjustment Fixture

T O MAKE PANELS USING VERTICAL panel-raising bits on a traditional router table, you have to slide the panels on edge along a
fence. This approach can be awkward, and the fence settings are hard
to replicate accurately.

I found that I could get better results by mounting the router horizontally, as shown. This fixture allows you to make extremely fine
height adjustments and accurate repeat settings. I made the wedge-
shaped section that holds the router from ¾-in. birch plywood. It
pivots on the edge of a bench. To use, loosen the three locking knobs,
adjust the router up or down with the adjustment knob and then
clamp the router in place with the three locking knobs. The weight of
the router keeps tension on the threaded adjustment rod. Markings on
the rim of the router piece allow adjustments (⅟₆₄ in. or less) and accurate repeat settings. Because travel at the rim is greater than travel at
the bit, you must widen the spacing between the adjustment marks.

—SID LADENSON, *Tustin, Calif.*

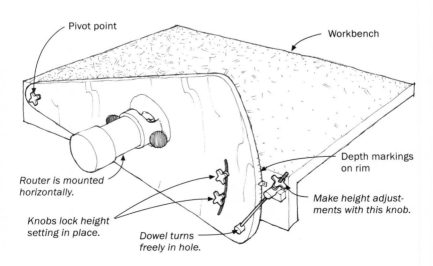

Pivot point

Workbench

Router is mounted
horizontally.

Depth markings
on rim

Make height adjust-
ments with this knob.

Knobs lock height
setting in place.

Dowel turns
freely in hole.

Clock Cavity Routing Jig

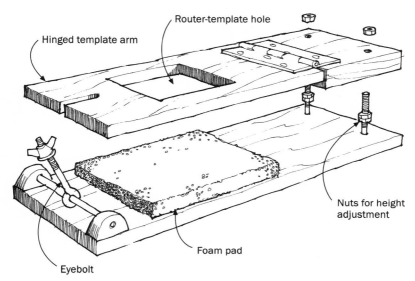

Router-template hole

Hinged template arm

Nuts for height adjustment

Foam pad

Eyebolt

ALTHOUGH I DEVISED THIS JIG for routing a cavity for a quartz clock works, the idea could be adapted to many routing operations. The beauty of the jig is that it combines a workpiece hold-down and a routing template in one device. It's well suited for small production runs because you can quickly pop workpieces in and out of the jig.

The jig consists of a base, a foam pad, the hinged template arm and an eyebolt. The eyebolt pivots on a bolt axle to fasten the template arm down over the workpiece. I attached the template arm to the base with bolts as shown in the sketch. The template arm can be set for the thickness of the workpiece by adjusting the nuts below the arm.

To use the jig, simply lay the workpiece on the foam pad, lower the template arm, lock it down with the wing nut and rout away.

—LES STERN, *Denver, Colo.*

Plunge Router Slotting Jig

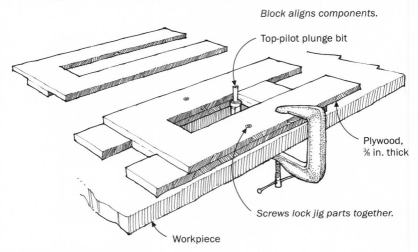

Block aligns components.

Top-pilot plunge bit

Plywood, ⅜ in. thick

Screws lock jig parts together.

Workpiece

Jig's two identical components slide together to set slot length.

I BUILD CABINETS FOR AUDIO, video and computer equipment. Each cabinet must be equipped with different-size access slots, depending on the equipment to be stored. To cut the various lengths of slots required, I came up with the router jig in the sketch. The jig, which I've found saves time and gives good results, is based on two interlocking, identical parts cut from ⅜-in.-thick plywood. A block glued to each U-shaped component aligns the pieces as they slide together. For best results, the pieces must fit together snugly.

To use the jig, slide the halves to the desired slot length, secure the assembly with two screws and clamp it down in the desired location. I use a plunge router with an Amana top-pilot (on the shaft) flush-trimming plunge bit, which has several advantages over a standard router fitted with guide collars or bushings. First, with a plunge router, you can rout the slot incrementally without having to stop and reset the cutting depth, and second, with a flush-trimming bit, you don't have to widen the jig slot to compensate for the collars. I have made several jigs for various slot widths, but the 1¼-in. width gets the most use.

—WARREN W. BENDER, JR., *Medford, N.Y.*

Cutting Hinge Mortises

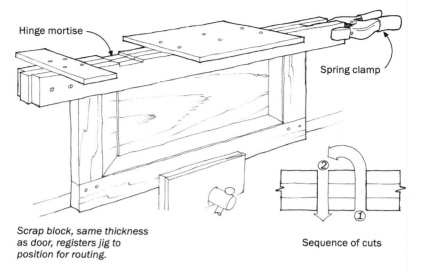

Hinge mortise

Spring clamp

Scrap block, same thickness
as door, registers jig to
position for routing.

Sequence of cuts

PERIODICALLY, I BUILD COLONIAL-STYLE KITCHEN cabinets with flush-mounted doors. One kitchen can have at least 20 or so doors with relatively small butt hinges mortised into the edge of each door. To cut the hinge mortises, I use a router and a simple jig made from scrap.

It consists of two arms spaced apart by a block the same thickness as the door frame. This spacer block also serves as a stop block in positioning the jig on the doors. I attach two ½-in. plywood fences to the top of the arms. The distance between the fences determines the size of the hinge mortises. Calculate this distance by adding the base of the router plus the width of the hinge minus the width of the mortising bit. Secure the jig to the door with a spring clamp.

To use the jig, put a door in the bench vise. Place the jig on the door with the stop block placed snugly against one end, and clamp it in place with the spring clamp. Set your router to a depth slightly less than the thickness of the hinge.

Reduce tearout by cutting the first and second passes, as shown in the drawing, and then clean out the remainder in the middle. Reverse the door in the vise, clamp the jig to the other end and cut the second mortise.

This jig is so easy to build that I don't bother to make it adjustable. I just keep one on hand for each size hinge I use.

—JEFF LIND, *South Berwick, Maine*

Centering Routed Mortises

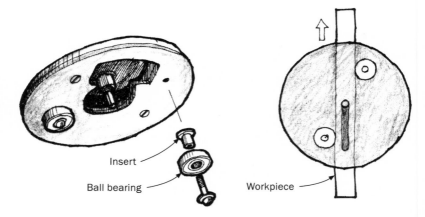

Insert

Ball bearing

Workpiece

H ERE'S A MORTISE–CENTERING IDEA I've used for quite a while. I use a plunge router to cut mortises in the stiles of frames. However, instead of the usual technique of using a fence to center the mortise, I attach two small ball bearings under the router base. On the Hitachi router I use (and most other routers), the subbase is attached with four screws. I remove two diagonally opposite screws and replace them with the bearing shown in the sketch. The bearing rides on a shopmade press-fit insert that is slightly longer than the bearing's thickness and that has an inner diameter to fit the bolt. The flange at the end of the insert can be machined as part of it, or it can be a separate washer. It need only be thick enough to prevent the bearing from rubbing on the router base.

In cutting the mortise, the bearings ride against the sides of the stile, automatically centering the mortise in the work. The size of the bearings is unimportant, as long as both are the same. Note that when cutting mortises near the end of the stile you must leave some extra length (I call it a "horn") for the bearing to ride on. Leaving a bit of excess to be trimmed off later is good practice, anyway.

—DAVID RING, *Yodfat, Israel*

[*Chapter 7*]

ROUTER JOINERY

Jointing Boards with the Router

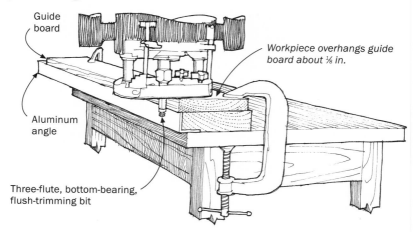

Guide board

Workpiece overhangs guide board about ⅛ in.

Aluminum angle

Three-flute, bottom-bearing, flush-trimming bit

I F YOU DON'T HAVE A JOINTER, this easy-to-use jig lets you joint boards with a router. The method depends on a simple aluminum-angle-edged guide board and a commercial-grade flush-trimming bit. I use the Bosch #85602M bottom-bearing, flush-trimming bit, which features three cutting flutes, a replaceable bearing and a 1½-in. cutting length.

To construct the jig, rabbet the guide board to receive the aluminum angle. Attach the angle to the guide board with countersunk screws every 6 in. or so. Now clamp the workpiece over the guide board so that it overhangs the aluminum-bearing surface by ⅛ in. or less. I like to use deep-throat Vise-Grip clamps to clamp the workpiece to the guide board, but C-clamps will work fine. If the workpiece is badly bowed, take two cuts or rip the board on the tablesaw first.

This concept has worked so well I made a smaller version for jointing the ends of crosscut boards. For this operation, it's important to double-check your depth setting to make sure the bit clears the angle. Also, take light cuts (less than 1/16 in.) to avoid burning the workpiece.

—ANDREW A. WESTERHAUS, *Burnsville, Minn.*

Jointing Long Boards with a Router

WHEN I NEEDED TO JOINT THE EDGES of several 12-ft.-long boards for gluing up a tabletop, I first tried using my jointer. However, even with auxiliary rollers on both ends of the jointer bed, I was not able to obtain a truly straight edge over the entire 12-ft. length. So I turned to this router-based method and achieved surprising success.

First, lay the long boards on the bench, good-side down, in the desired arrangement. Push the boards together as closely as possible, minimizing wide gaps between edges. Then screw several scrap cleats across the boards, putting at least two screws through the cleats into each board to keep the entire assembly from racking. Finally, scribe a few registration lines across the underside of the boards to assist later in glue-up.

When this assembly is complete, flip it over so that the good sides of the boards are facing up. Then, using a straightedge as a guide and a ¼-in.-dia. straight bit set slightly deeper than the thickness of the boards, rout down the middle of each gap between boards. This will remove stock from the edges of both boards, leaving a uniform gap between them. Remove the cleats, and glue up the boards as usual. The real beauty of this technique is that the straightedge used with the router does not have to be perfectly straight. Any slight waves or bows will be compensated for by an equivalent wave or bow on the other side.

—MICHAEL A. MASON, *Greendale, Wisc.*

Rout between boards to joint edges.

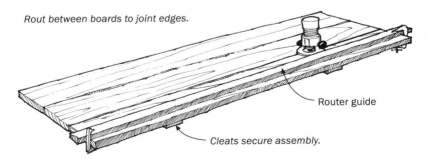

Router guide

Cleats secure assembly.

Aligning Glue-Joint Cutters on the Router Table

HERE'S THE METHOD I use to set the height of a glue-joint cutter above a router table. It allows boards of the same thickness to be run through and flipped side to side (not end for end) for a second pass on the other edge to yield an interlocking joint, aligning the boards' surfaces.

You must set the center of the glue-joint cutter to align with the center of the stock's thickness. The glue-joint cutter's center is midway along the center pitched line, an awkward point to gauge to. The cusps at either end of this pitched line provide much better reference points. On my cutter the vertical distance between these points is $\frac{1}{16}$ in. I set a marking gauge for half the thickness of the stock less half the pitch ($\frac{1}{32}$ in.). On the end of a short scrap I scribe two lines, one from either surface. The center of the stock is halfway between these lines, and they can be matched to the two cusps of the cutter.

I set the marked scrap on the router table against the infeed fence, touching the cutter, and align the two cusps of the cutter with the two scribed lines. With practice, it is possible to do this to an accuracy of $\pm\frac{1}{64}$ in. If closer alignment than this is necessary, a trial piece must be run and a minute adjustment made.

—JOHN GIBBONS

Router Setup for Edge-Jointing

THIS METHOD PROVIDES A QUICK and accurate setup for joining the edges of stock with a router. Make a two-piece jig that consists of an alignment fixture and a fence. The fixture sets the proper spacing of the boards. A single pass of the router shaves a little off each board. The best spacing is about ³⁄₃₂ in. smaller than the router bit. The fixture also sets the location of the fence. This is accomplished by cutting the two cross pieces the same length as the diameter of your router base.

To use the jig, set the two boards to be jointed on the bench with the alignment fixture between them. Slide the fence against the cross pieces of the fixture, then clamp the boards and fence to the bench. Remove the alignment fixture, and make one pass with the router to joint the two boards.

Once the jig is made and tuned, you can joint two boards in less than a minute. The resulting pieces will mate perfectly.

—JEFF COLLA, *Eden Prairie, Minn.*

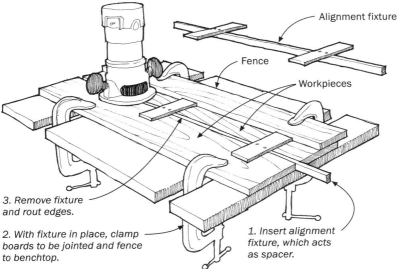

Alignment fixture

Fence

Workpieces

3. Remove fixture and rout edges.

2. With fixture in place, clamp boards to be jointed and fence to benchtop.

1. Insert alignment fixture, which acts as spacer.

Routed Box Joint

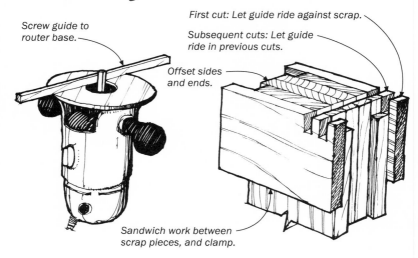

Screw guide to router base.

First cut: Let guide ride against scrap.

Subsequent cuts: Let guide ride in previous cuts.

Offset sides and ends.

Sandwich work between scrap pieces, and clamp.

I LIKE TO USE BOX JOINTS wherever I can because they look good, are strong and easy to assemble. I use a router to cut box joints, which is common, but my technique is a bit different. I have installed a guide block on the base of my router that acts as a jig for accurately spacing the finger cuts. The setup does not limit me in width, angle or length of project. I have made jigs to fit several common-size router bits but I usually prefer the ½-in. setup for most work. The sketch shows how to mount the guide block for ½-in. cuts. The accuracy of the joint depends on how carefully you position the guide in relation to the bit. Drill the screw holes in the router base a little large to give yourself some adjustment room.

To use the guide, sandwich the box sides and ends between two pieces of scrap, offsetting the sides from the ends ½ in. and the ends from the scrap ½ in., as shown. Now chuck a carbide bit in the router and make the first cut with the guide sliding against the scrap pieces.

For the second cut, just slide the guide in the newly cut groove. Continue the process across the ends of the boards for the rest of the cuts. It's like climbing a ladder. Wax the guide to slide easily in the grooves.

—GEORGE PERSSON, *Star Lake, N.Y.*

Routed Scarf Joint

WHEN I NEEDED TO MAKE SEVERAL scarf joints for a cover board in a boatbuilding project, I used a router and template to cut the joint's profile. The challenge was to shape the template so that the inside curve would be identical to the outside curve. Finally, I hit on the idea of using a router bit with the same radius as the joint's curve and a template bushing with twice the radius. With my router set up this way, all I needed for a template was a simple glued-up block with three straight-line edges.

—ROBERT L. THOMPSON, *New Hampton, N.H.*

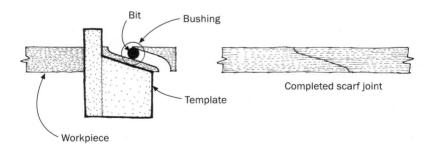

Bit
Bushing
Template
Workpiece
Completed scarf joint

Jig Cuts Slots for Corner Splines

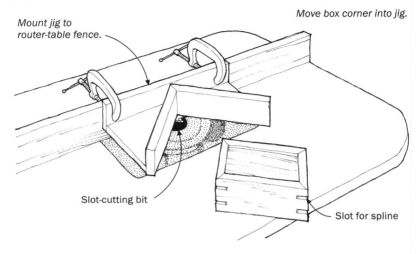

Move box corner into jig.

Mount jig to router-table fence.

Slot-cutting bit

Slot for spline

A COMMISSION FOR SIX IDENTICAL BOXES led me to develop this router-table jig for cutting spline mortises in outside corners. The jig is used with a slot-cutting bit. To make the jig, mount two 1x3s joined at a right angle to a backing board at a 45° angle. Clamp the backing board to the router-table fence so that the jig is directly above the bit. Adjust the fence in or out to get the right spline depth. To cut the slot, guide the box corner into the jig until it stops at the vertex. Using the jig, I can cut 48 slots in less than 10 minutes.

—MARK MAIOCCO, *Spotsylvania, Va.*

Cutting Clean Finger Joints
on a Router Table

I HAD BEEN TRYING TO CUT FINGER JOINTS in ¾-in. oak on the router table with a carbide-tipped straight bit. But the chatter was excessive and the joints splintered, even with a backer board. So I bought a high-quality, solid-carbide, spiral-fluted, up-cut bit. To my amazement, this bit wasn't much better than the straight one. It worked on oak, but when I tried it on softer woods like poplar and butternut, it burned the wood. Also, it left significant hanging edges in the entry and splintering at the back of the joint. This occured even with a lighter cut. I'm using a multispeed, 3½-hp router at 22,000 rpm.

Jeff Greef, who is an expert on the subject, told me that I needed a higher shear angle on the spiral. The low-angle spiral, found on many carbide bits, is not enough to prevent the rough chopping action that caused the chatter I was experiencing. He suggested I try using a steel end mill (available at machinist's supply houses) with flutes at about 45°. These metal-cutting tools are less expensive than solid-carbide bits and they cut wood very well.

Jeff also suggested using my tablesaw first to make relief cuts inside the slots where I was going to rout. One ⅛-in. saw kerf in each slot may be enough to significantly reduce the chatter.

Also, ½-in. slots are relatively wide and require the router bit to take a big bite with each cut. He suggested I try making the joints with narrower fingers. If I really want ½-in. fingers, it's better to set up on the tablesaw with a dado blade.

He also recommended using a fresh ¼-in. plywood backer board for each set of fingers. This will help prevent the splintering and the frayed edges.

—ALAN R. KIRK, *Cottage Grove, Minn.,*
and Jeff Greef, Santa Cruz, Calif.

Plate Joinery with a Router

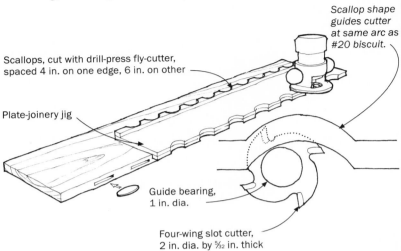

Scallop shape guides cutter at same arc as #20 biscuit.

Scallops, cut with drill-press fly-cutter, spaced 4 in. on one edge, 6 in. on other

Plate-joinery jig

Guide bearing, 1 in. dia.

Four-wing slot cutter, 2 in. dia. by ⁵⁄₃₂ in. thick

H ERE IS A ROUTER PLATE-JOINERY JIG for the budget conscious. This jig incorporates a series of scallops along both edges of a piece of Baltic birch plywood to eliminate the tedious clamping and unclamping required when cutting a series of biscuit slots with a single-slot jig.

To construct the jig, start with a piece of plywood about 10½ in. wide and 42 in. long. Using a fly-cutter in a drill press and a fence, bore a series of equally spaced 3-in.-dia. holes, just touching each edge. I spaced the scallops 4 in. apart on one edge and 6 in. apart on the other to provide a variety of slot spacings. Now glue and clamp ¼-in. by 1-in. strips of plywood along the diameter of each line of holes on opposing faces of the jig. When the glue has cured, rip equal amounts off each side, leaving ⅜-in.-deep scallops and a fence on the edges. This size scallop, when used with a 2-in.-dia. wing cutter and a 1-in.-dia. guide bushing, will produce an arc that will cut a semicircular slot matching a #20 biscuit size.

To position the jig, line up the centerline with a centerline scribed on the edge of the workpiece.

—R. BRUCKEN, *Martinez, Calif.*

Single-Setup Routed Drawer Joint

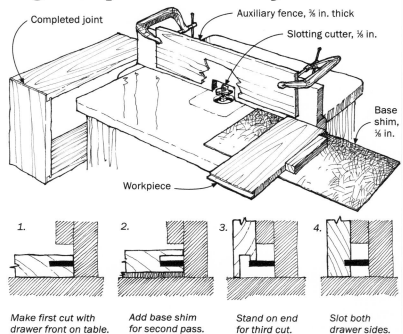

Completed joint

Auxiliary fence, ⅜ in. thick

Slotting cutter, ⅛ in.

Base shim, ⅛ in.

Workpiece

1. Make first cut with drawer front on table.

2. Add base shim for second pass.

3. Stand on end for third cut.

4. Slot both drawer sides.

H ERE IS A SINGLE-SETUP SOLUTION for routing tongue-and-rabbet drawer joints. The setup uses a standard ⅛-in. slotting cutter chucked in a router that's mounted under a router table. You'll also need a piece of ⅛-in.-thick Masonite for a base shim and a length of ⅜-in.-thick material for an auxiliary fence. Adjust the height of the cutter so the slot starts ½ in. above the router table, and adjust the fence so the slot's depth is a shade over ½ in. (this is usually the full depth of the cutter). Clamp the auxiliary fence to the main fence, ¾ in. above the table, so a ½-in. drawer side and the base shim can slide underneath.

The sequence of cuts is shown in the sketch. Three passes will produce the tongue and rabbet on the drawer fronts and backs. One pass will produce the groove on the drawer sides. Although it's not shown, you can also use the same setup to groove the drawer sides to receive the bottom. Screw the auxiliary fence to the tool's fence so you can remove the clamps for clearance and make two passes, one against the table and another using the base shim. The result will be a ¼-in. groove ⅛ in. from the bottom of the drawer side.

—BRAD SCHWARTZ, *Deer Isle, Maine*

Routing Spline Slots in Mitered Frames

THIS SIMPLE LITTLE JIG is extremely useful for routing blind spline slots in spline-mitered frames. Nail or glue together scraps of the frame lumber into the configuration shown. The workpiece should fit accurately into the slot, where it can be pinched in place with a clamp. A plunge router is desirable, both for ease of starting the cut and because it has a built-in fence for centering the slot. A regular router will do if you add an integral fence to the jig itself by tacking on more scraps, shimmed with cardboard where necessary. I scribed marks on the jig to show where to start and stop.

—JIM SMALL, *Newville, Pa.*

Rout slot in workpiece for spline.

Make jig from offcuts of work to be joined.

Routing Through Mortise-and-Tenon Joints

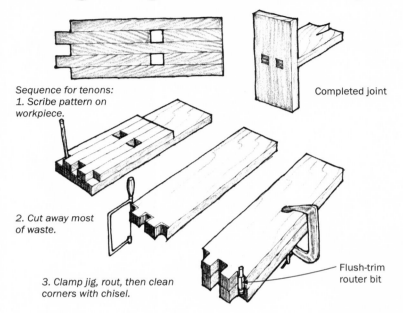

Sequence for tenons:
1. Scribe pattern on workpiece.

Completed joint

2. Cut away most of waste.

3. Clamp jig, rout, then clean corners with chisel.

Flush-trim router bit

I DESIGNED THIS ROUTER JIG to produce accurate, repeatable through tenon joints.

The jig consists of strips of MDF laminated together as shown in the drawing. The long, continuous pieces correspond to the spacing between mortises. The shorter pieces are glued up to form openings and projections that correspond to the thickness of the stock.

To use the jig, place it over the workpiece to be mortised (or tenoned) and pencil in the outline of the joint. Remove most of the waste. Now clamp the jig in place under the workpiece so it becomes a guide for the bearing of a flush-trim router bit. This results in clean, accurate mortises or tenons with straight sides except in the corners, which must be cleaned up with a chisel.

—ED DEVLIN, *Rothsay, Minn.*

Miter-Joint Biscuit Jig

THIS JIG, WHICH I DESIGNED to cut mitered biscuit slots with a router, has eliminated my struggles with miter joints. It consists of a hardwood base, which bolts to my workbench, and an angled Plexiglas slide, sized to fit my router base.

To cut the slot, I use an Eagle-American biscuit cutter that has a ball-bearing limiter. The short shank on these bits limits the distance the cutter can be safely extended from the chuck. You can center the biscuit slot in ¾-in. stock; in thicker stock, you'll have to accept a biscuit slot nearer to the outside of the joint.

Mounting the 45° Plexiglas slide is critical because the recess in the Plexiglas must fit the mitered corner of the workpiece perfectly. To aid in this assembly, place a mitered workpiece in the jig to register the Plexiglas in the right position as you mark the mounting holes. Make the mounting holes slightly oversized, so you can adjust the slide if necessary.

—FRANCIS CHAN, *Nassau Bay, Tex.*

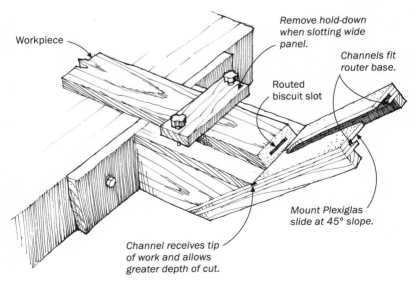

Workpiece

Remove hold-down when slotting wide panel.

Channels fit router base.

Routed biscuit slot

Mount Plexiglas slide at 45° slope.

Channel receives tip of work and allows greater depth of cut.

Slot-Cutting Jig for Splined Miter Joints

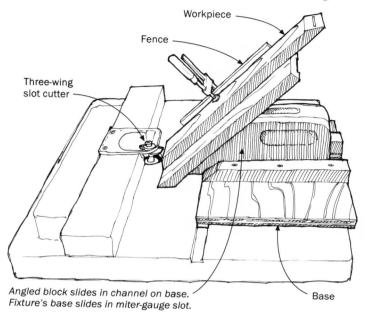

Workpiece

Fence

Three-wing
slot cutter

*Angled block slides in channel on base.
Fixture's base slides in miter-gauge slot.*

Base

I'VE FOUND THAT EXPENSIVE slot-cutting machines aren't really
needed for plate joinery. A ⁵⁄₃₂-in.-wide, three-wing slot cutter
mounted in a router table works well. To use the router for edge-to-
edge plate joinery, hold the right end of the work securely as you
push the edge into the cutter and rout a slot slightly longer than the
biscuit.

Cutting the spline slots for mitered frames, however, is not quite so
easy and requires a special fixture like the one shown in the drawing.
The fixture's base rides in the router table's miter-gauge slot. Two
pieces of 1¼-in. by 1¼-in. stock are screwed to the base to form a

channel perpendicular to the miter-gauge slot within this channel; a
block of wood with one end cut at a 45° angle slides toward or away
from the three-wing cutter. Finally, a board with a fence screwed to
one edge is mounted on the angled surface of the block to register the
workpiece and provide a clamping perch.

To use the fixture, clamp the mitered workpiece on the 45° block
and push it into the cutter. You can cut a longer slot by moving the
base of the carriage in the miter-gauge slot. Make pencil marks on the
base of the workpiece to designate the ends of the slot; in production
situations, clamp stop blocks to the top of the router table to limit the
length of the slot.

—JIM CHRISTO, *Jamestown, N.Y.*

Keyed Miter Joints

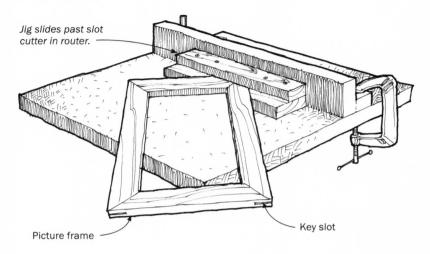

Jig slides past slot cutter in router.

Key slot

Picture frame

I LIKE TO REINFORCE THE MITER JOINTS in my picture frames by adding a contrasting key after the glue in the joint has set. The usual method of cutting the key slot is with a tablesaw and a vertical 45° jig riding on the fence, but I find it easier and safer to make the cut on the router table with a slot-cutting bit.

The jig, shown in the sketch, can be made in just a few minutes and has the advantage of enclosing the spinning bit throughout the operation. The resulting slot has a flat bottom and is uniform in width. Inexpensive bits are available to cut slots as narrow as $\frac{1}{16}$ in., which looks better on a small frame than the $\frac{1}{8}$-in. slot produced by a tablesaw's blade. On larger frames, I cut two slots by setting the bit a little below the centerline, cutting the first slot and then flipping the frame over for a second pass.

—PAUL DAVIS, *Lake Stevens, Wash.*

Routing Slots

S LOTS FOR THE SPLINES in miter joints can be cut neatly and quickly with a router and a straight bit (carbide-tipped works best).
With the depth of cut set to one-half the width of the spline plus
½ in. for excess glue, rest the base of the router on the face of the
miter. Adjust the router fence (a block clamped to the router base will
probably work better) so the outside edge of the miter will guide the
bit as it cuts the slot. Using as a pivot the point where the outside
miter edge meets the corner formed by the router base and the fence,
lower the bit into the face of the miter and cut the slot. This method
cuts the slot parallel to the edge of the miter, which helps the spline
compensate for cup in the board. Also, the cut can be started and
stopped without exposing the spline at either end of the joint.

—DAVID LANDEN, *Chapel Hill, N.C.*

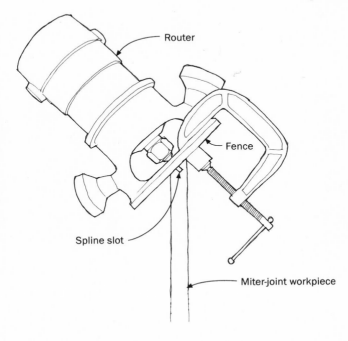

Router

Fence

Spline slot

Miter-joint workpiece

Routed Miter Joint

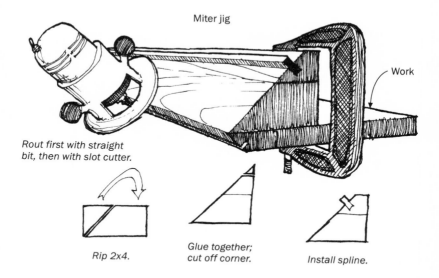

Miter jig

Work

Rout first with straight
bit, then with slot cutter.

Rip 2x4.

Glue together;
cut off corner.

Install spline.

I RECENTLY HAD TO MAKE TWO 24-in.-long, splined 45° miter joints to join a coffee-table top to its sides. Since the tabletop was too large for me to use my tablesaw, I devised a way to cut miters and spline grooves with my router and a simple homemade jig. To make the jig, select a 2x4 slightly longer than the required joint and, using a carbide-tipped blade for smoothness, rip the board at 45°. Glue and screw the smaller piece to the main piece to extend the face of the jig, as shown in the sketch. Rip a ¼-in. groove a little less than 3 in. from the pointed edge of the jig and install a spline in the groove. The spline serves as a straight-edged guide for the router's base.

To use the jig, rough-cut the workpiece at 45°, leaving it about
⅛ in. long. Position the jig exactly on the cut line and clamp in place.
Chuck a double-fluted carbide bit in your router and feed the router
along the jig slowly and carefully. The ends are especially delicate. After
the mitering cut is complete, leave the jig in position, chuck a slot
cutter in the router and rout the spline slot. For a blind spline just stop
the cutter an inch or so from the end. Repeat the process on the
matching 45° piece. If the jig is made accurately, you'll be amazed how
perfectly the joint will turn out.

—PAUL DARNELL, *Phoenix, Ariz.*

Routing Splined Miter Joints

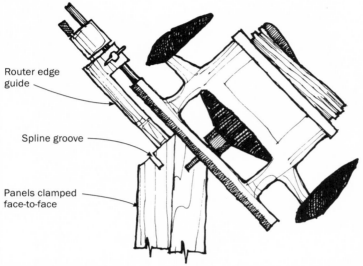

Router edge guide

Spline groove

Panels clamped face-to-face

T HIS ROUTER-BASED METHOD for cutting the slots in splined miter joints is easy to set up and guarantees an accurate fit. First miter the panels in the normal fashion on the tablesaw and clamp them face-to-face as shown in the drawing. Wide or bowed panels may require the addition of a stiffener clamped below the miters. Now chuck a splined-sized bit (⅛ in. or 3⁄16 in. for ¾-in. stock) into the router and set the depth of cut (¼ in. to ⅜ in.). Adjust the router guide to be about ¾ in. from the bit. It is not necessary to have absolute accuracy in depth and guide settings. Rest the base of the router on the peak formed by two panels and rout a spline slot in each panel. To cut a stopped spline slot, just plunge the router.

Although the whole process can be accomplished with little more than eyeball measurement, the right angle formed by the two miters and the constant offset of the cut all but guarantee success.

—WARREN H. SHAW, *San Francisco, Calif.*

Jointing Mitered Segments with a Router

WHILE MAKING A ROUND SUNBURST mirror frame consisting of 16 segments, I had to miter both sides of each segment at precisely 11¼° on my tablesaw to get a gap-free fit. Rather than trust the accuracy of the saw cut, I came up with another approach.

I started by cutting each segment as close as I could to the proper angle and then glued up four segments at a time to form the four quadrants of a circle. I then positioned one quadrant at a time on a perfectly square board so that an equal amount of the quadrant overhung each edge of the board. I clamped the quadrant in place and trimmed off the overhang, using a flush-trimming bit in my router.

When all four of the quadrants were trimmed in this way, I dry-fitted them to check for a tight joint that would require minimal clamping pressure. No further trimming was needed, but if it had been, I would have glued up two semicircles and trimmed the edges with a straight board.

—ANTHONY FUDGE, *Snow Hill, Md.*

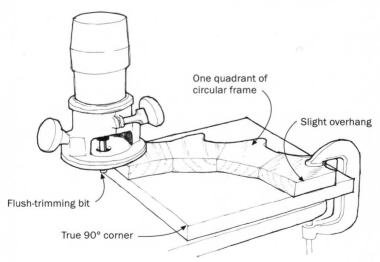

One quadrant of circular frame

Slight overhang

Flush-trimming bit

True 90° corner

Routing a Scarf Joint in Plywood

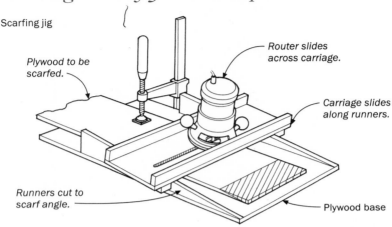

Scarfing jig

Plywood to be scarfed.

Router slides across carriage.

Carriage slides along runners.

Runners cut to scarf angle.

Plywood base

I N OUR BOATBUILDING SHOP, we've used several types of router jigs to scarf plywood. The jig pictured in the sketch is easy to make and to use. It consists of two wedge-shaped runners cut at the same ratio as the scarf ratio required. These are mounted on a piece of ¾-in. plywood or a workbench. A router fitted with a wide plunge bit rides on a carriage resting on those runners. The plywood to be scarfed is clamped between the runners. By sliding the board along the runners, the router cuts a perfect scarf.

When scarfing plywood, an 8-to-1 ratio is required if using epoxy glue. So a scarf in ½-in. plywood would be 4 in. long. If you use another type of glue, cut your scarfs at a 12-to-1 ratio (6 in. in ½-in. plywood) to be safe.

The best discussion of scarfing plywood that I've read is in *The Gougeon Brothers on Boat Construction* (Gougeon Bros., Inc., P.O. Box 908, Bay City, MI 48707; 517-684-7286).

—CHRIS KULCZYCKI, *Arlington, Va.,*
from a question by S. J. Hetzel, Safety Harbor, Fla.

Making Tenons on Chair Rungs

HERE'S HOW TO USE YOUR ROUTER TABLE to produce tenons on the end of chair rungs quickly and accurately. First, chuck a rabbeting bit into the router and raise it until the bit's bottom is even with the top of the router table. I locate a V-block near the bit to produce the diameter desired, and clamp the V-block in place using the router table's fence. Then, holding the rung firmly with one hand, lower it into the rotating bit. Rotate the rung with the other hand in a counterclockwise direction. The result will be a clean and uniform reduction of the dowel diameter. To reduce splintering, take several small bites of ⅛ in. or less.

—DAVID J. LANGLEY, *Corvallis, Ore.*

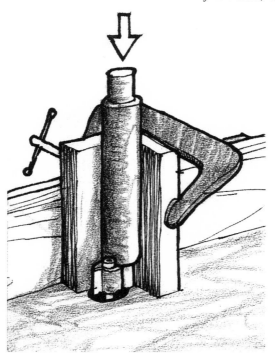

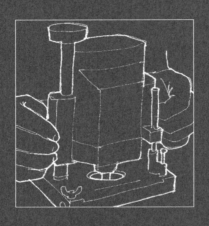

Chapter 8

FIXTURES
FOR CURVED &
CIRCULAR WORK

Router Circle-Cutting Jig

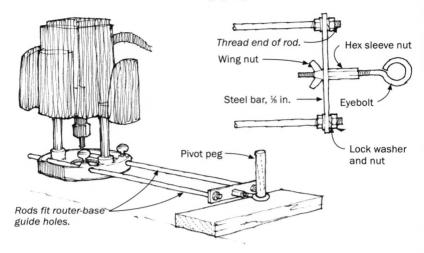

Thread end of rod.

Hex sleeve nut

Wing nut

Steel bar, ⅛ in.

Eyebolt

Pivot peg

Lock washer
and nut

Rods fit router-base
guide holes.

T HIS INEXPENSIVE but accurate circle-cutting jig is made with two
18-in.-long rods that fit the guide holes in your router. Cut
threads on one end of each rod and, using nuts, attach the rods to a
length of ⅛-in.-thick steel bar, as shown above. Take care to ensure that
the rods are parallel and spaced the right distance apart. For the pivot,
attach an eyebolt to the center of the steel bar with a hex sleeve nut
and a wing nut. For the center (pivot) peg, I use a ¾-in. dowel, shaved
down slightly to fit the center of the eyebolt.

—JAMES GUERAMI, *Lake Forest, Calif.*

Circle Guide for the Router

THIS FIXTURE FOR ROUTING CIRCLES has several advantages over commercial circle guides: It's cheaper, it cuts circles smaller than the router base and it allows repeat setups to precise radii without trial and error.

The guide is easy to make. Screw a piece of ¼-in. plywood to the base of your router, carefully countersinking the screws. The plywood should be as wide as your router base and somewhat longer than the largest radius you intend to cut. Saw or drill a clearance hole for the router bit.

For a 4–in. radius circle, for example, measure out 4 in. from the edge of the bit and drill a small hole at that point. Insert a brad in the hole, point up, to serve as a pivot. Drill a center hole in a piece of scrap, place it on the guide, rout a short arc and measure the radius produced. You'll be lucky if it is right the first time. Regardless, label that hole with whatever radius it produces (say, 4¹⁄₁₆ in.). Then make another hole closer or farther, as the case may be, until you get the radius you want. Remember to mark each hole as you go.

Since the markings are accurate for only that particular bit, you can divide the guide into sections and head each group of holes with the bit used—½-in. straight, for example.

—BRIAN J. BILL, *Old Bridge, N.J.*

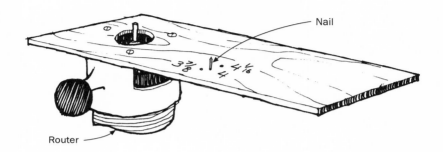

Making Disks on the Router Table

T O CUT SMOOTH, accurate circles, make a sliding wooden strip to fit in the miter-gauge slot of your router table. The strip should protrude just slightly above the surface of the table so a clamp will hold it in place. Put a screw through the center of the workpiece into the wood strip. The screw should be just loose enough so the work will rotate. The screw can be driven up through the strip and into the bottom of the work if you don't want a visible hole. Turn the piece counterclockwise to make the cut, and slide the strip right or left to adjust the radius. The size of the disk can range from 8 in. or so to about 24 in., depending on the router table.

—TOM RAUSENBERG, *Dayton, Ohio*

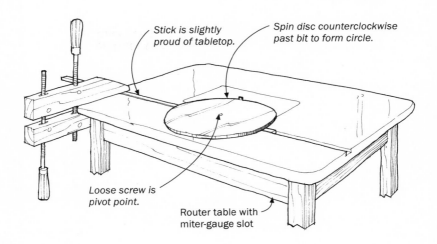

Stick is slightly proud of tabletop.

Spin disc counterclockwise past bit to form circle.

Loose screw is pivot point.

Router table with miter-gauge slot

Router Circle Cutting, Simplified

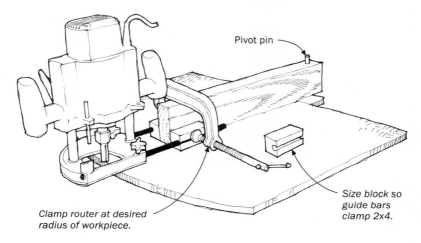

Pivot pin

Clamp router at desired
radius of workpiece.

Size block so
guide bars
clamp 2x4.

ALTHOUGH I'VE SEEN DOZENS of methods for routing circles over 40 years of woodworking, the method I stumbled on many years ago is still the least complicated and quickest I've seen.

Two small hardwood blocks kept right in the router storage case are the heart of the method. The blocks slip on your router's guide bars leaving a bit of the bar exposed, as shown in the sketch. When the blocks are in position, the distance between them should be 1⅜ in., the thickness of a 2x4, so that any length ripped from a 2x4 can be used to size the radius of the circle to be cut.

To cut the circle, drill a ¼-in. pilot hole in the 2x4, and use a dowel or ¼-in. bolt on a block as a pivot. Or just drive a nail through the 2x4 if the hole won't show. Adjust the router so the bit is in position; then clamp the 2x4 between the blocks and the guide bars with a C-clamp. The open holes in the blocks allow the pads on the C-clamp to pull up tight on the guide bars without slipping off. With this system, you can rout circles as small as 6 in. to as large as…now let's see, what's the length of a 2x4?

—TIM HANSON, *Indianapolis, Ind.*

Milling Radiused Corners on Tabletops

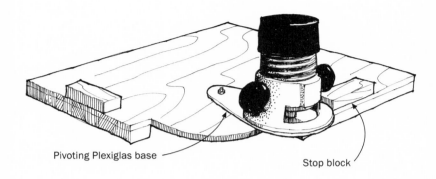

Pivoting Plexiglas base

Stop block

ACED WITH THE PROSPECT of milling 80 identical-radiused corners on a run of restaurant tables, I came up with the "Corner King" jig shown in the sketch. It's built from a square of ¼-in. plywood, with fences attached to the bottom on two sides. A pivoting Plexiglas arm was designed to allow a ½-in. router to swing through the proper radius (4 in. in this case). Adding stop blocks to the top limited the travel of the bit to 90°.

A nice feature of the jig is that the first pass with the router cuts the jig's plywood base into a perfectly radiused pattern. In practice, I set the jig on a corner, trace the radius pattern directly off the base, remove the jig and trim the bulk of the waste with a jigsaw. Then, I screw the jig to the tabletop and use the router to finish the corner.

—AL DORSA, *St. Croix, Virgin Islands*

Radiused Corners on Countertops

I LIKE TO PUT A RADIUSED CORNER on any countertop that projects into a traffic area: The corner won't hurt as much when you bump into it. This simple jig, used with a scrap block and a plunge router with a round base, helps me cut the corner quickly and accurately. For plastic-laminate counters, I cut the corners of the core before applying the laminate.

Measure the distance from the edge of your router base to the cutting edge of a straight bit placed in the chuck. Cut an L-shaped piece of plywood with each leg the same width as the bit-to-base distance. Attach fences to the long sides of the jig so that it will butt square against the corner of the countertop.

With the jig held in place on the corner, nail or screw a scrap block to the countertop core. Remove the jig, and make light cuts with the router against the block, plunging ¼ in. at a time to cut the radius.

—JOHN BOUSFIELD, *Cocoa, Fla.*

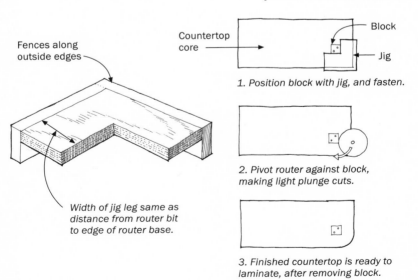

Fences along
outside edges

Countertop
core

Block

Jig

1. Position block with jig, and fasten.

Width of jig leg same as
distance from router bit
to edge of router base.

**2. Pivot router against block,
making light plunge cuts.**

**3. Finished countertop is ready to
laminate, after removing block.**

Routing a Raised-Rimmed Tabletop

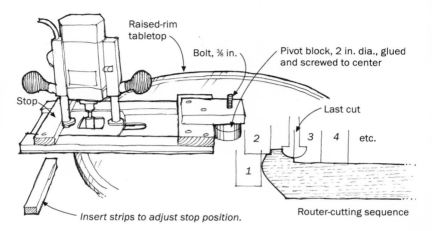

Raised-rim tabletop

Bolt, ⅜ in.

Pivot block, 2 in. dia., glued and screwed to center

Stop

Last cut

2 | 3 | 4 | etc.

1

Insert strips to adjust stop position.

Router-cutting sequence

I N REPRODUCING AN 18TH–CENTURY PEDESTAL TABLE, I was faced with the problem of forming a raised-rim top. The traditional method was to use a lathe for this process. But even my small 25-in. top was far beyond the capacity of my lathe. So I devised this router jig to shape the table's top.

First, I cut the top to the required diameter on a bandsaw and then screwed a pivot block holding a countersunk ⅜-in. bolt to the center of the top. The sinking was to be ⁵⁄₁₆ in. deep, so I made sure the pivot block's screws only penetrated ¼ in. Then I made the fixture to pivot on the bolt. With a two-flute straight bit in the router, I initially used the setup to true the edge of the top to a perfect circle; I made subsequent cuts from the outside in. To avoid having to move the stop for each cut, I inserted spacing strips to position the router for up to four sweeps of the jig before I had to reposition the stop.

When as much of the sinking as possible had been done in this way, I used a core-box bit to form the cove on the rim. To sink the central part of the table, I removed the pivot block and lengthened the base of the jig to span the width of the top. Finally, I smoothed the entire recessed top with a plane and a scraper.

—DR. RALPH SINNOTT, *Wolverhampton, England*

Recessing Tabletops with a Router

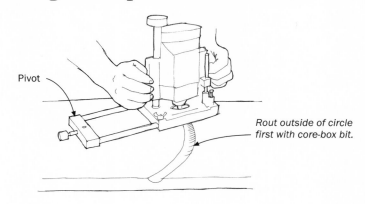

Pivot

Rout outside of circle
first with core-box bit.

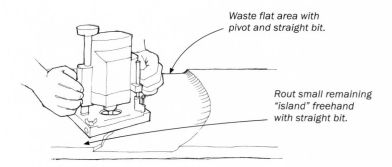

Waste flat area with
pivot and straight bit.

Rout small remaining
"island" freehand
with straight bit.

FOR RECESSING LARGE BOWLS and tabletops, a router setup is safer and faster than turning the large workpiece on the lathe, especially for beginners or for woodworkers who own light lathes. In the sketch you can see how the router method works. For demonstration purposes, I'm routing a dish in a wide board. Of course, the wood would be larger if I were making a bowl or a tabletop.

You need a router that has at least ½ hp, and it should accept ⅜-in. or ½-in. shank bits. Smaller routers won't work so well because the ¼-in. shank bits they take snap off. I use a Makita router with two bits, a carbide-tipped two-flute straight cutter and a core-box (round-end) bit. To make a pivot pin, I drilled a hole in the top of the router fence and threaded it for a ³⁄₁₆-in. stovebolt. The bolt should stick out a little less than the depth to which you want to rout. A nut on the inside of the fence keeps the pin from unscrewing. If a larger diameter is needed, extend the fence with steel rods.

To rout your board, drill a hole in the center to accept the pin. Don't go too deep, though, or the hole will show when you're done. If I were making a finished piece, I'd rout the outside of the circle first, taking several shallow passes instead of one deep one, to keep the wood from burning and the bit from vibrating too much. You could skip this step, as I did, and bandsaw the circle round later on.

Next, do the inside edge. If you want the sides of your bowl to join the bottom in a radius, make the inside cut with a core-box bit of the right diameter. Put the straight bit back in the router and continue wasting material, working toward the center in ¼-in. passes until you can't move the router any closer. A circle about 7 in. in diameter will be left in the center.

Remove the fence and, holding the router freehand, rout away as much wood as you can. As the island of wood in the middle gets smaller, holding the router level will be harder, so be sure to leave enough for the router base to rest on. Be very careful—one slip will ruin all your work. To remove the last of the high point, use a handplane or a chisel or both, followed by a scraper for final smoothing.

—TAGE FRID,
from a question by Mark R. Westerman, Frontenac, Kans.

Hole Cutter for Speaker Enclosures

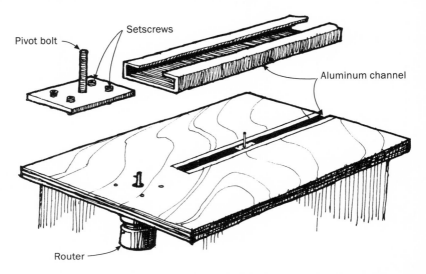

I HAVE BEEN INVOLVED IN MAKING PROFESSIONAL sound equipment and speaker enclosures for a number of years. The usual construction routine requires me to cut holes up to 18 in. in diameter for speaker baffles. Here's how I use a modified router table to cut the holes accurately, quickly and safely.

My router table is constructed of ⅜-in. Baltic birch plywood. I've installed an aluminum-channel track and pivot assembly on the centerline of the table as shown in the sketch. The standard 1½-hp Makita router bolted underneath the table is equipped with a stagger-tooth cut-out bit (Wisconsin Knife Works #68802).

To cut a circle on the setup, I first slide the pivot assembly to the right position for the radius I want. Then I lock the assembly in place by tightening the four setscrews. Next, I drill a centerhole in the baffle board and slide this over the pivot assembly's threaded rod. I secure the baffle board with a flat washer and a self-locking nut. The baffle board should rotate on the pivot with a mild resistance. I then turn on the router, bring it up through the wood and rotate the baffle clockwise on its pivot point to cut a perfect circle. Once the device is set, you can quickly reproduce duplicate baffles.

—JAMES CAMPBELL, *Orange, Calif.*

Router Jigs for Making Molding

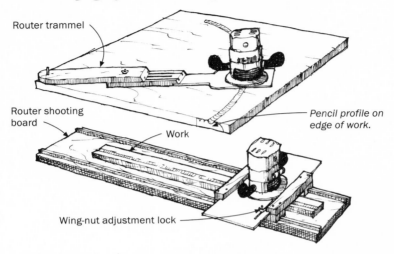

Router trammel

Router shooting board

Work

Pencil profile on edge of work.

Wing-nut adjustment lock

THE SKETCHES SHOW TWO JIGS that, when used with a portable router, can produce both semicircular and straight molding in patterns difficult to produce with a shaper. The first jig is an adjustable router trammel used to make curved molding. The jig's two-part base adjusts by means of a slot-and-track arrangement and locks with a bolt and wing nut. The router is screwed to a ¼-in. hardboard foot, which is, in turn, screwed to the base.

The second jig consists of a sliding adjustable router holder and a "shooting board" that has two parallel tracks. The slotted hardboard in the holder allows the router to be adjusted laterally.

To use these jigs, first pencil the molding profile on the edge of the workpiece. Position the work and the jig so the router is right over the molding. Take repeated cuts adjusting the bit depth, changing bits and adjusting the router's lateral position as needed. When all the routing is complete, separate the curved molding from the waste stock with a bandsaw. Some sanding is necessary to finish the molding.

—S. GAINES STUBBINS, *Birmingham, Ala.*

Making Bending Molds from Router-Cut Plywood

WHEN I MADE SOME PLYWOOD forms to laminate a curved headboard, I discovered this trick. If you cut the forms with a router bit the same diameter as the thickness of the laminated workpiece, you will automatically have the slightly different curves needed for the inside and the outside molds. They will fit perfectly when clamped up.

To make a matched pair of bending forms, screw a wooden bar to your router base to act as a trammel. Mark a centerline on a sheet of plywood, and lay out the locations of the slots. Rout the arcs, leaving a small piece uncut at the end of each radius to hold the sheet together. When done, cut the pieces to size. Stack the cut parts for inside and outside molds, and screw them together.

—KEN SHAW, *San Diego, Calif.*

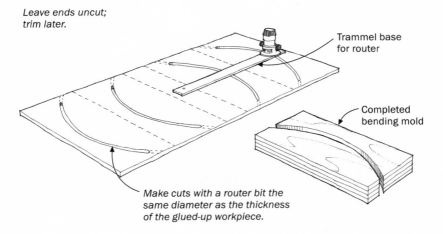

Leave ends uncut;
trim later.

Trammel base
for router

Completed
bending mold

Make cuts with a router bit the
same diameter as the thickness
of the glued-up workpiece.

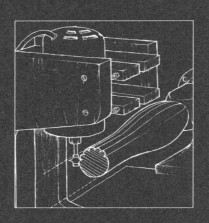

FLUTING, REEDING, & MILLING

Fluting Jig for Tapered Legs

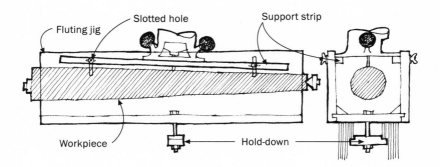

Slotted hole — Support strip — Fluting jig — Workpiece — Hold-down

T HIS JIG ROUTS ACCURATE and consistent flutes on tapered turned legs. The jig is a U-shaped plywood channel as wide as your router base, mounted to the lathe bed. Dimensions will vary according to your router base and the peculiarities of your lathe bed. Attach two router-support strips to the inside of the jig with bolts and wing nuts through slotted holes, so the strips can be angled parallel with the tapered leg.

To use the jig, first turn all legs to shape, then mount the jig to the lathe bed. Chuck one leg between centers, locking it into position with the index head. Now set the router-support strips parallel with the turned workpiece. To do this, simply set a board (as wide as the interior of the jig) on the work, and tighten the support strip's wing nuts with the strips resting on the board. Remove this adjustment board and fasten stops to the support strips, so each flute will be the same length. Now you're ready to rout the flute. Use the holes in the lathe's indexing head for accurate spacing of the flutes around the leg.

—JOHN SANFORD, *Camden, Maine*

Fluting Fixture for Short Columns

F LUTING IS AN OPERATION so seldom required that it does not warrant buying special equipment for the purpose. So when I needed to flute some short columns, I made this fluting fixture from a laminate trimmer, hardwood scraps and Plexiglas. The construction details shown in the sketch can easily be modified for your particular needs.

—HARRY J. GURNEY, *Taunton, Mass.*

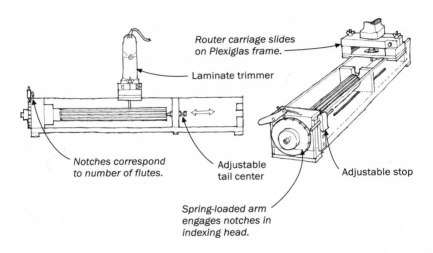

Router carriage slides on Plexiglas frame.

Laminate trimmer

Notches correspond to number of flutes.

Adjustable tail center

Adjustable stop

Spring-loaded arm engages notches in indexing head.

Fluting Flat Surfaces

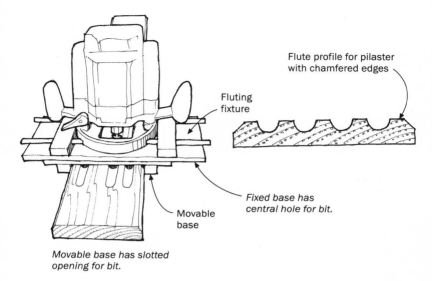

Flute profile for pilaster with chamfered edges

Fluting fixture

Fixed base has central hole for bit.

Movable base

Movable base has slotted opening for bit.

FLUTING IN FLAT SURFACES adds grace to fireplace surrounds, doorway casings and the like. This router jig simplifies the process.

Start by building a guide carriage with two parts: a fixed base that attaches to the router and a movable base that straddles the workpiece. I used ⅜-in.-thick Baltic birch plywood, but any similar dense material will do. It is possible to fasten the two parts of the jig together with wing nuts and slots. But because there are usually only two settings, I screw the two parts together with six wood screws.

Tradition dictates four or five flutes. I like to use four flutes because I can get the maximum effect with the minimum of router settings. Either way, lay out the profile of your flutes on a piece of paper to determine spacing (the layout shows you the settings for the jig). Remember that you will be making identical cuts from both edges of the workpiece, so only two settings will yield four flutes. Draw index marks on the fixed base to show where you will attach the movable base.

Get the feel of your jig by making practice runs on a scrap cutoff.
Take note of the following:

- The movable base must straddle the stock so that it slides freely but
  with minimal slop in the fit. This requires the stock to be perfectly
  uniform in width.
- Use new or freshly sharpened core-box bits. Dull bits are hard to
  push and leave burn marks.
- Check the spacing of the flutes with only two of the six base
  screws in place. Adjust the settings of the movable base if necessary.
  When the spacing is perfect, screw the movable base to the fixed
  base with all six screws.
- Use a variable-speed router, if possible, and slow the speed at either
  end of the flute.
- Draw the router toward you. Make several passes, and finish with a
  fine cut.
- Use a good respirator mask and a pair of goggles.

—WILLIAM D. LEGO, *Rockford, Ill.*

Grooving Square Tapered Legs with a Router

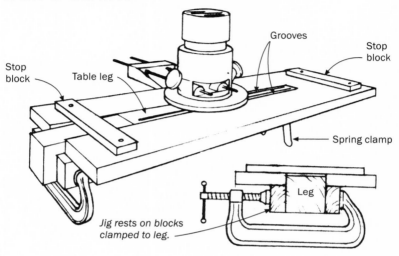

THE BEST WAY TO CUT STOPPED GROOVES into square, tapered legs is with a router. Use a small veining bit, which cuts a semicircular groove. Build a plywood jig that fits over the tapered leg. This will give you a good bearing surface for the router base. To guide the router fence, taper the long edges of the jig to match the leg taper. Fasten stop blocks at each end of the jig as shown, so that the router base bumps into them and stops the cut at the right point.

Since the leg tapers, setting up the jig requires some fussing. Clamp the leg in a vise (the folding workbenches from Sears or Black & Decker are great because they can clamp irregular shapes). Line up the jig so the surface of the plywood is flush with the leg's tapered surface. To support the jig, clamp scrap blocks on one end of the leg and a spring clamp on the other.

—SIMON WATTS, *Berkeley, Calif.,*
from a question by E. F. Bell, Medford, Ore.

Routing V-Grooves in Tongue-and-Groove

TO PRODUCE IDENTICAL CHAMFERS on matching edges of tongue-and-groove stock, I use an extra piece of stock with a nailed-on router fence, as shown in the sketch. Both the tongued and the grooved edges can be pushed flush to the jig, ensuring a balanced V-groove in the finished work and eliminating the extra setup that would be required with a shaper or a tablesaw. You could adapt the idea to a router table just as easily.

—W. A. WARD, *Underbill, Vt.*

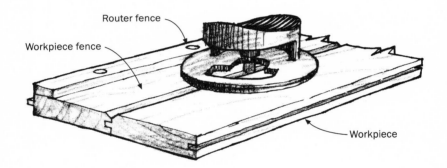

Router fence

Workpiece fence

Workpiece

Quick Setup for Routing Grooves

R ECENTLY, I HAD TO ROUT some slots at odd angles for a display rack. Here's the method I devised. Lay out the grooves on the project, and draw a centerline through each one. Make a rectangular base for your router from ¼-in.-thick clear plastic by scribing a center-line through the base centered on the bit. Then trim both edges 3 in. away from the centerline. You can now use the base like a drafting template to set up the router.

To use the base, retract the bit below the base. Set the router over the centerline of the groove, and place a guide bar against the plastic base, parallel to the cut line. Clamp the guide bar in position, 3 in. away from the centerline. If the grooves are stopped, you can add stops to the guide bar. Mine are two L-shaped pieces of wood tightened with a bolt and wing nut.

—RICHARD HERST, *Redondo Beach, Calif.*

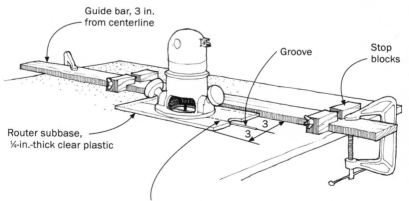

Guide bar, 3 in. from centerline

Groove

Stop blocks

Router subbase, ¼-in.-thick clear plastic

3

3

Scribe centerline on bottom of rectangular base.

Routing Stopped Grooves for Inlay Strips

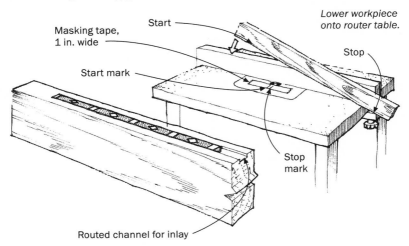

Lower workpiece onto router table.

Masking tape, 1 in. wide

Start

Start mark

Stop

Stop mark

Routed channel for inlay

WHILE I WAS PREGNANT with our first child, my husband, Marty, and I made a crib. In addition to using the wood of our choice (maple), we wanted to personalize the crib with inlay strips. But we needed to find a place where the inlay would survive a baby's inquisitive fingers and teeth. For safety, we centered the inlays in the top of each drop-side rail under plastic teething protectors.

Choosing the inlay pattern from Rockler Woodworking and Hardware (4365 Willow Dr., Medina, MN 55340; 800-279-4441; www.rockler.com), we bought strips for the two rails, each ¼ in. wide by 36 in. long, plus extra length so the pattern would match at the ends. To create stopped grooves for the inlay strips, Marty used his router table, setting the depth of cut to 0.075 in., half again the ½₀-in. thickness of the inlay. The extra depth kept the strips (with glue) below the top of the rail, which let us buff out the finish without damaging the inlays.

To show where to start and stop each cut, he laid a strip of masking tape on the table in front of the router bit. Setting a square against the fence and against the edge of the router bit, he marked off both sides of the ¼-in. straight-cutting bit. Then he made corresponding start and stop marks on the side of the two top rails (see the drawing). The marks allowed him to see where the bit's edges were while the work was covering them.

To start each cut, Marty plunged the rail onto the router bit with the workpiece start mark in line with the tape's leading bit mark. He guided the work along the fence and then ended the cut by lifting the piece off when the tape's trailing mark and the rail's stop mark aligned.

—Barbara Bazemore, *Merrimack, N.H.*

Routing Reeding on Turned Bedposts

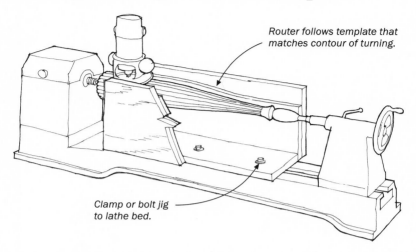

Router follows template that matches contour of turning.

Clamp or bolt jig to lathe bed.

R EEDING CURVED, tapered bedposts is not easy. Commercial furniture makers do it with special dedicated tools. In the home
shop, you can set up a router on your lathe with an indexing device
on the headstock and a jig as in the drawing.

Some lathes have a built-in indexing wheel that locks the headstock
at 5° increments, or you can jury-rig one by attaching an old saw-
blade or other toothed wheel to the headstock spindle. Make the
reeding template by bandsawing two pieces of thin stock (say, ½ in.) to
a contour that matches the cross section of your turning. Then nail or
screw these pieces to the stock that will form the sides, and mount the
assembly on your lathe. The exact height of the sides will vary from
lathe to lathe, and each turning, unless it's a duplicate of an original,
will require its own template.

When you're setting up, make sure the bit tracks exactly on the radial line along the center of the turning, or else the flutes will be skewed. It's best to make a test-turning of the same size to try out the jig before tooling the actual workpiece.

This method has limitations. The curve of the column cannot be too radical or else the router base will rock and produce an uneven cut as it's pushed along. And no matter how the reeds are cut, the small end of the turning will have narrower, faceted reeds, which you will have to shape by hand-sanding or with a flap-wheel sander. Reeds that stop at a bead or other detail must be completed by hand with chisels or gouges.

Off-the-shelf router bits don't work very well for this job. They're usually too wide at the rip or the radius is not quite the right size. I grind my own bits from a commercial steel bit that is close to the profile I need or from a broken bit.

—R. PERRY MERCURIO AND RICHARD HEISEY, *Winchester, Va.,*
from a question by Don Carkbuff, Plainfield, Ill.

Reeding on Turned Bedposts

HERE'S A BETTER METHOD for reeding turnings, be they straight or curved. You need a custom-made router bit, available from Fred Velepec (71-72 70th St., Glendale, NY 11385). I mount the router in a plywood jig, as shown in the drawing. Then, I rig a wooden spring latch to my lathe that engages the holes in the indexing wheel, locking the headstock for the router operation.

A cove turned at both ends of the reeded section allows the bit to exit and enter cleanly, so that no hand cleanup work is needed.

—JAMES B. SMALL, *Newville, Pa.*

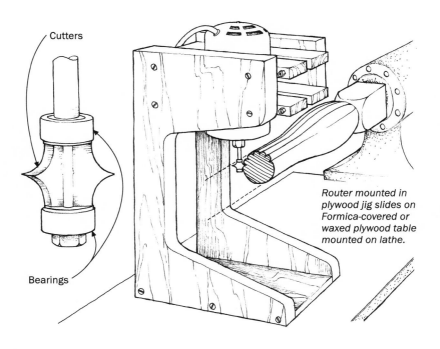

Cutters

Bearings

Router mounted in plywood jig slides on Formica-covered or waxed plywood table mounted on lathe.

Edge Detail on a French Armoire

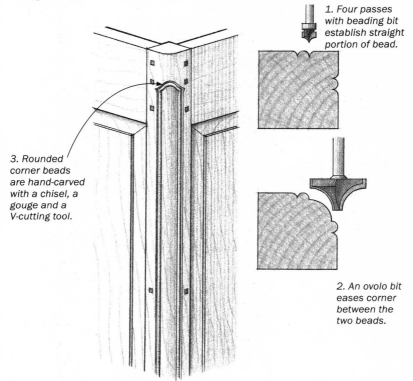

1. Four passes with beading bit establish straight portion of bead.

3. Rounded corner beads are hand-carved with a chisel, a gouge and a V-cutting tool.

2. An ovolo bit eases corner between the two beads.

ERE'S HOW I CUT THE EDGE detail on the French-styled armoires I build. The corner post of the armoire features a rounded corner lined on each side with a small bead. This detail keeps the case from appearing too boxy and lends a light look to the hefty armoire. I used a series of stopped router cuts, then carved out the top and bottom details by hand.

I first drew out the design with a pencil, making sure to mark the top and bottom portions where the design starts to curve and where the router cuts stop and the handwork begins.

For each of the two small beads, I loaded the router with a beading bit (Eagle #1390602) and used a fence to guide two parallel cuts on each face of the post. I stopped the bit just short of the rounded sections on the top and bottom. I used a ⅜-in. ovolo bit to relieve the sharp corner between the two beads. Again, I guided my cut with a fence and watched my marks to make sure I stopped short of the top and bottom.

For the curved details on the top and bottom, I used a V-cutting tool to define the bead. A straight chisel and a slightly contoured gouge were used to finish the rounding on the corner.

It took some patience to get the detail just right, but after the piece went together, it proved to be a small touch that made all the difference.

—CHRIS GOCHNOUR, *Salt Lake City, Utah,*
from a question by John Testerman, Menifee, Calif.

Hot-Glue Surfacing Sled

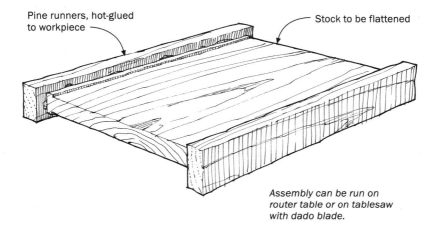

Pine runners, hot-glued to workpiece

Stock to be flattened

Assembly can be run on router table or on tablesaw with dado blade.

HERE IS A QUICK SURFACING method I conceived to salvage a badly misshapen piece of beautifully figured walnut that I wanted to use for a cribbage board. I first jointed the two long edges of the warped walnut and then fastened two pieces of scrap pine to these edges with hot-melt glue, thereby creating a sled with the walnut centered between the two pine runners. To make sure the assembly was square, I held the three pieces together against the fence and top of my tablesaw while the glue set. The hot glue is strong enough to hold the sled together during milling, sets up in minutes and enables easy disassembly when the operation is finished.

I used the sled to flatten the walnut by running it on a router table, but it would work just as well on a tablesaw fitted with a dado blade or molding head. With each fence setting, I made four passes by turning the sled over and swapping it end for end.

—TOM ROSE, *Los Angeles, Calif.*

Flattening a Workbench Top

I RECENTLY COMPLETED MY FIRST WORKBENCH, a large traditional design with a heavy laminated maple top. After assembly, I flattened the top of the bench using the method described below.

First, I installed a ¼-in.-thick Lexan plastic subbase on my router. Then I screwed 1x2 fir strips down each side of the bench, extending the strips far enough past the ends so I could rout the entire length. To make sure these two runners were parallel, I used two winding boards. Then, using scrap maple, I made a sled that bridged the tabletop and incorporated grooves for the Lexan router base. To surface the table, I simply started at one end and, with a ½-in. bit in the router, cut ⅟₁₆ in. in a pass. It is a little slow, but it works.

—HERB HUNTER, *Denver, N.C.*

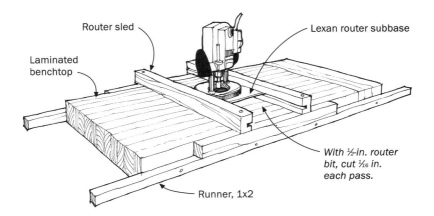

Router sled

Lexan router subbase

Laminated benchtop

With ½-in. router bit, cut ⅟₁₆ in. each pass.

Runner, 1x2

Surfacing Small Pieces with a Router

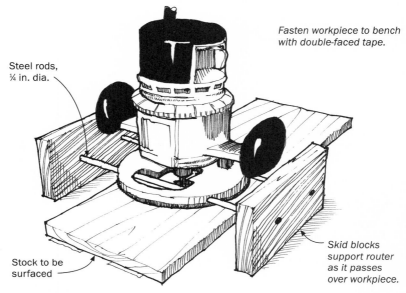

Fasten workpiece to bench with double-faced tape.

Steel rods, ¼ in. dia.

Stock to be surfaced

Skid blocks support router as it passes over workpiece.

I RECENTLY NEEDED TO THICKNESS–PLANE some small pieces of cherry to make a box. I don't have a planer, but I did the job quite satisfactorily using my router and the simple jig shown in the sketch.

To make the jig, run two ¼-in.-dia. steel rods through the guide holes in the router base. Tap the ends of the rod into 14-in.-dia. holes bored into two wooden skid blocks that are large enough to hold the router above the workpiece to be surfaced. Then, chuck a ¾-in.-dia. carbide-tipped straight bit in the router.

Before using the jig, resaw the workpiece to the approximate thickness that you need, and fasten the wood to the benchtop, rough side up, with double-faced tape. Then move the router jig over the rough surface of the board, taking a light cut with each pass. It only takes a short time to surface and thickness the workpiece.

—RICHARD ADLER, *Gulf Breeze, Fla.*

Shaping Beams with a Router

FOUR YEARS AGO MY EIGHT-YEAR-OLD DAUGHTER, an aspiring gymnast, pleaded for a balance beam of her own to practice on. Her request made it necessary to find a way to shape the sides of a 16-ft. beam into uniform arcs, so that the finished beam would be as near regulation size and shape as possible. My solution was a sliding jig that guided a router with a 1-in. bit. The jig consists of two parts: the sliding base and the router carriage.

Curved rails on these parts guide the router in the proper arc. In laying out the jig you must increase the radius of the curved rails by the amount that the bit protrudes from the router base so that the end of the bit follows the desired finished radius. I recommend you lay out the plan of the jig full-size to verify the correct juxtaposition of beam, cutter and jig.

To use the device, start at one end of the beam and arc the router to and fro as you slide the jig along. The router will let you know how much of a bite to take. The process is slow but accurate. To finish up the very ends of the beam, where the bit can't reach, you can rig up some additional bearing surface or simply use a chisel and plane.

—BURT BABKES, *Eugene, Ore.*

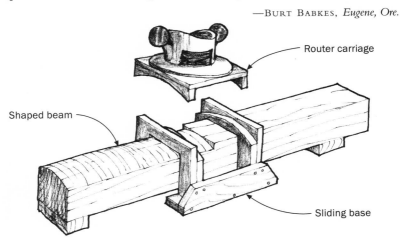

Router carriage

Shaped beam

Sliding base

Milling Large Surfaces

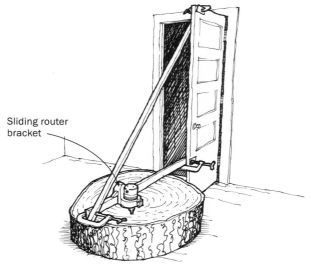

Sliding router
bracket

HERE IS THE PROCEDURE I used to accurately mill the surface of a 4-ft.-dia. 288-year-old ponderosa-pine section destined for a museum exhibit. I utilized the shop door as a swinging vertical axis to which I clamped a horizontal beam and a diagonal brace, as shown in the drawing. I made a mounting bracket for the router so it could slide along the beam and be locked in position anywhere. Marks along the horizontal beam designated increments slightly less than the diameter of the surfacing bit I was using so I would know how far to move the router after each pass.

To use the rig, I leveled the tree section on the floor near the shop door. Then, I turned on the router and swung the beam and router assembly back and forth across the workpiece, moving the router one increment after each completed pass. I got the best results by swinging the beam first from right to left and then from left to right on each pass. On the first swing, the pressure from the cut raises the router slightly out of the workpiece; then on the back swing the router removes just a whisker, producing an accurate surface requiring only sanding. If you aren't getting a flat surface, your door jamb is probably out of plumb.

—LAWERENCE I. JAYNE, *Davenport, Wash.*

Surfacing Log Slabs with a Router

HERE'S A LOW-COST FIXTURE for surfacing end grain on crosscut slabs.

—MARK BASHAM, *Chula Vista, Calif.*

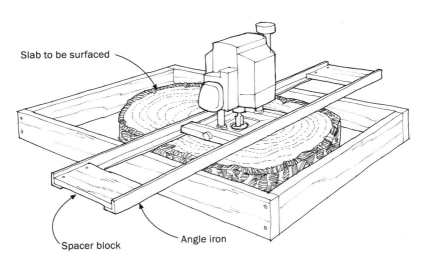

Slab to be surfaced

Spacer block

Angle iron

ROUTER METHODS & ODD JOBS

Preventing Tearout
when Routing Drawer Fronts

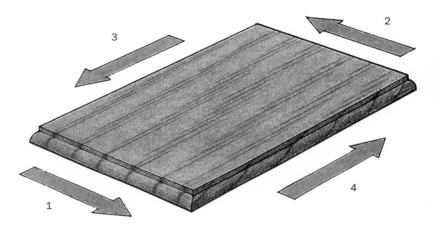

Avoiding tearout: Tearout generally occurs at the end of a cross-grain cut because the fibers at the end of the cut are not supported. If you rout across the grain first, tearout can be routed away with the long-grain cuts.

ROUTED DRAWER FRONTS typically require a rabbet and a thumbnail. A common problem is chipping of the wood at the corners. There are several things you can do to reduce or prevent this problem.

When removing a lot of material, it is better for the wood, the bit and the router to take a number of small passes, rather than one pass at full depth. I would probably rout the rabbet in three passes and the thumbnail in two, routing the thumbnail first. Use sharp bits, and always test sample boards before routing an actual workpiece.

I also suggest routing your drawer fronts on a router table instead of using a handheld router. Pushing a workpiece across a table and against a long fence is a much more stable situation than trying to keep a handheld router balanced on a small drawer front and a short fence tight up to the edge of a drawer front.

Perhaps the most important thing you can do is to rout the ends before the long sides. Wood tends to tear out at the end of a cross-grain pass, so by routing across the grain first, then with it, you can usually rout away any chipping that occurs at the corners (see the drawing).

To eliminate the possibility of tearout at the corners, you can support the back edge of the workpiece. I like to use a miter gauge with an auxiliary wooden fence to keep the work at right angles to the fence. Then I attach a backup stick to the auxiliary fence, using double-faced tape, and butt the workpiece against this backup stick. The backup stick should be the same thickness as the drawer front, at least ¾ in. wide and long enough to support the work firmly.

If you don't have a miter-gauge slot on your router table, you can keep the drawer front at right angles to the fence by pushing it along with a wide, squared-up piece of wood or plywood that rides against the fence.

—LYNETTE BRETON, *Rockport, Maine,*
from a question by Edward J. Hessler, Kalamazoo, Mich.

Reducing Tearout on Toy Parts

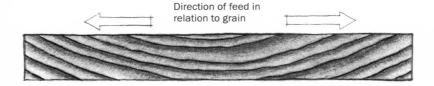

Direction of feed in
relation to grain

MANY TOYMAKERS LIKE TO USE A ROUTER and a rounding-over bit to make toy parts safer and to give them greater definition. But since you're encountering every kind of grain when you go around the irregular workpiece, it is common to experience torn and ragged cuts in places. Here are some suggestions for reducing tearout.

Conventional practice calls for routing counterclockwise, as this keeps the bit from self-feeding, digging into the cut and bogging down. But there are situations when routing clockwise is desirable. Tearout and splintering occur frequently when routing end grain; so look at the way the fibers are arranged on the end-grain edges and move the router in the direction these fibers run. This may mean that on the same end grain you'll rout first in one direction and then in another.

Taking too deep a cut can also cause chipping. Make several shallow passes before taking a very light, final cut, especially light if you are routing clockwise. A sharp bit will leave a smoother, crisper edge. Carbide-tipped bits with ball-bearing pilots are best for your purpose.

—FINE WOODWORKING EDITORS,
from a question by Alec R. Colvos, Tacoma, Wash.

Trimming Plastic Laminate without Scratches

W HEN WORKING WITH PLASTIC laminate sometimes the pilot
bearing of the laminate-trimming bit gets gunked up with
contact cement, causing the bearing to spin and scratch the plastic
laminate. This is primarily caused by cutting out a piece of laminate
much larger than the substrate, which forces the bit to wade through a
large area of laminate and glue. So the first thing to do is to cut the
laminate so it will overhang the substrate as little as possible; ¼ in. all
the way around should be enough. Extending the cutting edge of the
bit below the glueline (as far as you dare) also helps keep glue out of
the bearing.

Another way to prevent the pilot bearing from seizing up and causing scratches is to keep the bearing, as well as the laminate surface that
guides it, free from the buildup of partially dried contact cement. A
rag with a little naphtha or mineral spirits will do the trick. There's
also a product called TRIM-EASE (available from American Grease
Stick Co., 800-253-0403) that's designed to keep pilot bearings from
gunking up. Just rub this stick lubricant along the path of the bearing.

When all else fails, switch to a flush-trimming bit fitted with a Del-
rin sleeve. This nylonlike plastic sleeve covers a standard metal pilot
bearing, making it less likely to cause scratches. These bits were developed for routing solid-surface countertop materials, such as Corian
and Avonite, without damaging the surface. You can purchase Delrin-
sleeved bearings individually from Eagle America (P.O. Box 1099,
Chardon, OH 44024; 216-286-9334). Just make sure the outside
diameter of the bearing you buy matches the cutting diameter of the
flush-trimming bit you're working with.

—PHILIP SMITH, *Long Beach, Calif.,*
from a question by John Hayns, Whangarei, New Zealand

Raising Panels with Router Outriggers

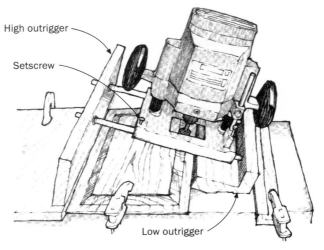

High outrigger

Setscrew

Low outrigger

I WANTED TO MAKE SOME RAISED PANELS, but I didn't want to invest in a shaper and special cutters. My solution was to raise the panel with a ¾-in. two-flute helical end mill in my router. All that's needed is a simple jig to tilt the router base to 15°. I fitted two pairs of ¹⁵⁄₃₂-in. drill rods (four rods in all) through the existing holes in my Makita router base. I then epoxied a low outrigger to the outboard side and a high outrigger to the inboard side. The low outrigger acts as a fence against the edge of the panel. In the sketch, the tongue that will fit the frame's groove has already been milled on the tablesaw, but you could just as well do this step afterward.

The high outrigger rides atop the panel or, if the panel is narrow (as in the sketch), atop a board of the same thickness clamped to the bench. By using four rods you can remove the outriggers from the router. But if you need to rout a different panel profile, you will need to make up another set.

—EDWARD M. ROSENFELD, *Gunley, Ala.*

Hinged Router Fixture for Raising Panels

THIS ROUTER FIXTURE is great for quickly and safely beveling panels. It's made from ¾-in. plywood and some scraps. Its table is hinged and adjusts via a slotted support arm to vary the bevel angle.

I use a ½-in.-dia. carbide bit and make three passes. The first two passes remove the bulk of the stock. The final pass removes only about ⅟₃₂ in. of material and leaves a clean face without ripples.

—GERALD ROBERTSON, *Angus, Ont., Canada*

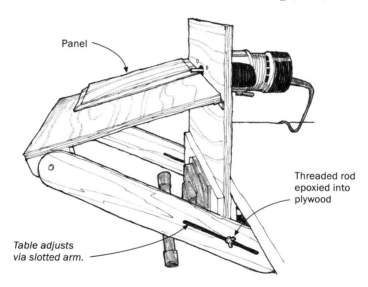

Panel

Threaded rod
epoxied into
plywood

*Table adjusts
via slotted arm.*

Routers Preferred for Raising Panels

F OR RAISING PANELS, I prefer the router over the tablesaw, radial saw, jointer or shaper—it is much easier and more accurate to pass a router over a panel than to feed the panel into the cutter of a stationary machine, unless you have an industrial-grade power-feed mechanism to move the panel.

If you're a serious woodworker, I would recommend you consider a large, high-horsepower plunge model for raising panels. The router's weight and mass serves to dampen vibration and increases stability. Increased power means the router won't lug down under load. The bit's rpms stay higher and the resulting cuts are smoother with less tearout and burning. The larger units can also accept bits with ½-in. shanks, which vibrate less than their ¼-in. cousins. Increased bit size also tends to have a "flywheel effect," generating greater momentum for the cutter and a steadier cut. The ½-in. bits are also available in such a variety of shapes that they can make the router as versatile as any shaper.

There are several methods for raising panels with a router. Many companies offer panel-raising cutters. Until a few years ago, these bits were the kitchen cabinet-door variety with bevels of ½ in. to ¾ in. Specialty grinding houses, quick to fill the demand created by the new generation of plunge routers, now offer panel cutters suitable for upscale furniture. These bits with ball-bearing pilots sell in the $100-plus range and can cut bevels and contours up to 1½ in. wide. Since these bits can be up to 3½ in. in diameter, manufacturers urge caution in their use and suggest they be used with some type of router table. Basically, this "under-the-table router" is a shaper and subject to the same inherent dangers and safety considerations as a shaper.

Before investing in these larger bits, check with the router manufacturer to make sure the bits are compatible with your machine. On some
models, the resistance of the larger bits might cause the motor bearings
to overheat and could destroy the armature as well, via heat transference.
Also, the increased ampere draw would generate heat of its own, resulting in damage to, or failure of, various motor components.

Aside from specially designed bits, panels can also be raised using
conventional double-fluted straight bits with a handheld router and
appropriate jigs. The jig must be designed to regulate the bit feed laterally and vertically, so that wood can be removed gradually in controlled
increments. These straight bits have the advantage of being modestly
priced and can be used for other jobs besides raising panels. The only
disadvantage is speed. But even though the large raising bits are faster,
their cost, limited application, risk to the router, and the skill and expertise needed to use them make them unsuitable for most workers.

One final note: eye, ear and dust protection should always be worn
when using any router.

—BERNARD MASS, *Edinboro, Pa.,*
from a question by John Kelly, Overland Park, Kans.

Making Dowels with the Router

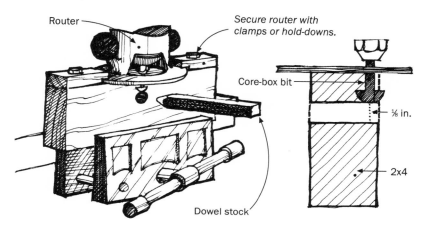

Router

Secure router with
clamps or hold-downs.

Core-box bit

⅛ in.

2x4

Dowel stock

HERE'S HOW TO MAKE DOWELS of any size with a simple router
setup. First, drill a pilot hole through a 2x4 the same diameter
as the dowel you want to produce. Chuck a core-box bit in your
router, rout a recess in the front of the 2x4 just above the hole and
clamp the router in position. Center the bit right over the top of the
hole with the shaft of the bit inset about ⅛ in. into the 2x4. Make sure
the leading edge of the bit is precisely at the circumference of the
hole. Now turn on the router and push the dowel blank into the hole,
rotating the blank with a hand drill. Taper the front of the blank for
easier starting.

—G. WELDON FRIESEN, *Middlebury, Ind.*

Making Long Dowels

I NEEDED A ¾-IN.-DIA. OAK DOWEL more than 6 ft. long to use as a curtain rod. Unable to find supplies, I came up with a method to make the dowel in my shop without a lot of effort.

First, I rounded the edges of a 7-ft.-long, ¾-in.-thick oak board with a ⅜-in. corner-round bit in my router. I didn't round over the first and last 6 in. of the board because I knew I'd need the square ends for a clamping surface later. Moving the board to the tablesaw, I set my fence at ¾ in. and ripped off the rounded edge. I then flipped the stick over, clamped it back to the board with three quick-action clamps (for stability) and rounded the top and bottom edges to produce a dowel. Of course, I had to reposition the middle clamp to finish the rounding. When I trimmed off the two square ends, I had my long dowel, ready to scrape, sand and finish.

—PHIL LISIK, *Hemlock, Mich.*

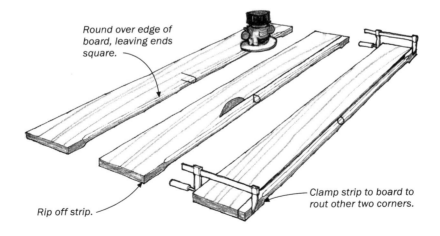

Round over edge of board, leaving ends square.

Rip off strip.

Clamp strip to board to rout other two corners.

Making Dowels with the Router and Lathe

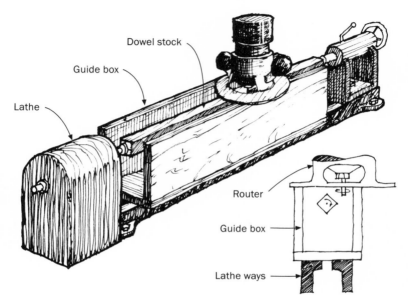

Dowel stock

Guide box

Lathe

Router

Guide box

Lathe ways

H ERE'S HOW TO MAKE DOWELS on your lathe with a router. First build a guide box with sides a little higher than the turning stock. Allow about an inch of clearance between the stock and the box walls. Chuck a ¼-in. straight bit in your router and adjust the depth of cut, so that when the bit is over the dowel stock it will cut the dowel about ⅟₁₆ in. oversize. Position the router on the downward side of the stock rotation as shown in the sketch. Turn on the lathe, turn on the router and cut away. Take several light cuts to reduce the possibility of the bit grabbing and breaking the dowel. Lower the bit to the final depth and make one final pass with the router centered over the dowel.

—LEE R. WATKINS, *Littleton, Colo.*

Router-Based Lathe Duplicator

I'VE HAD GOOD RESULTS WITH THIS SIMPLE router-based lathe dupli-
cator that consists of a rigid, open-ended plywood box that can be
attached firmly to the lathe bed between centers. The top of the box is
a flat surface on which your router rides.

The box should be sized so its top just clears the maximum diameter you wish to turn, and a 2-in. to 2½-in. straight bit can reach
downward far enough to make a shearing cut off the side of the spindle. I made my top surface with Masonite—a fixed piece on the operator's side and a removable, shaped template piece on the far side,
against which the router collar bears.

Start with round or octagonal stock and work the spindle down to
its finished diameter by making several passes from the tailstock to
headstock. Run your lathe at its slowest speed. Simple duplicators like
this are best for reproducing gradual diameter changes, but do so in
such a quick and foolproof manner that they allow plenty of time for
any hand-turned detail work you might desire.

—DAVID SCOTT, *Clyde, N.C.,*
from a question by David Haynes, Nanooske, B.C., Canada

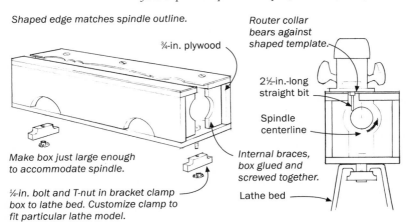

Shaped edge matches spindle outline.

¾-in. plywood

Router collar
bears against
shaped template.

2½-in.-long
straight bit

Spindle
centerline

Make box just large enough
to accommodate spindle.

Internal braces,
box glued and
screwed together.

¼-in. bolt and T-nut in bracket clamp
box to lathe bed. Customize clamp to
fit particular lathe model.

Lathe bed

Making Tapered Cylinders without a Lathe

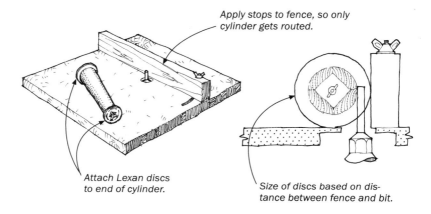

Apply stops to fence, so only cylinder gets routed.

Attach Lexan discs to end of cylinder.

Size of discs based on distance between fence and bit.

I USE A ROUTER TABLE to make tapered cylinders for kaleidoscopes, but the method could be adapted to make table legs or large dowels. I start by gluing up four pieces of wood into a column. Then I attach two ¼-in. Lexan plastic circles to the ends of the column using a threaded rod and wing nuts. If the workpiece is solid, you can attach the circles with screws. I press the assembly against the router-table fence and make repeated passes, turning and sliding, to produce the cylinder. Stops on the router-table fence keep me from routing into the circles.

Note that two equally sized circles produce a straight cylinder and unequally sized circles produce a taper. The circle should be larger than the cylinder by the distance of the router bit from the fence. In my case, I use 5-in. and 4½-in. circles to cut cylinders that taper from about 3 in. to 2½ in.

—JOHN GRANT, *Palmer, Alaska*

Pocket-Making Jig for a Router Table

HERE'S A ROUTER-TABLE TECHNIQUE to produce clean, precise pocket holes for joining face-frame members. First, construct a wooden cradle fitted with a lever-operated toggle clamp. The cradle angles the workpiece as pocket holes are milled. To cut the pockets, mount a straight-cutting bit in the router, and with the workpiece clamped in the fixture, slide the fixture along the fence on the router table. A stop clamped to the fence prevents the pocket from running out the end of the workpiece.

To complete the pockets, drill screw-shank-sized holes from the end of the board to meet the pockets. Face-frame assembly is simple. Just clamp the stiles and rails together with glue, and drive screws through the pockets.

—PAUL K. MURPHY, *San Jose, Calif.*

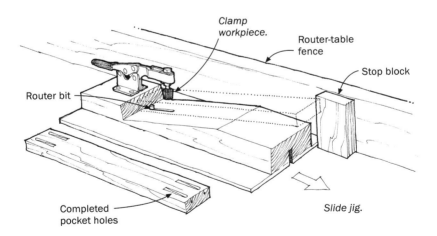

Clamp workpiece.

Router-table fence

Stop block

Router bit

Completed pocket holes

Slide jig.

Cutting Pocket Holes
with a Router-Table Ramp

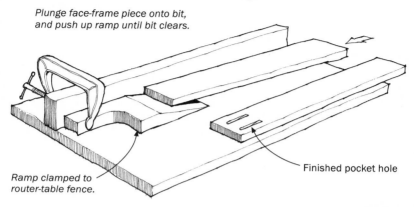

Plunge face-frame piece onto bit, and push up ramp until bit clears.

Finished pocket hole

Ramp clamped to router-table fence.

NOT TOO LONG AGO, I went down to the tool store on a wishing trip. I saw a pocket cutter, which I really don't need for the five or six screw pockets that I cut in a year. But something pushed my Rube Goldberg button, and I rushed back to the shop to build a complicated pocket-cutting contraption that used an old router suspended from a shaft like a pendulum. Well, after I cut pockets in all my scrap lumber, I began to wonder "Now what do I do with the machine—put it on a shelf to collect dust?"

About this time, the Goldberg fever left me, and I remembered something my dad told me: "Maybe you don't need another machine. Just figure out how to do the job with something you already have." So after some thought, I came up with a markedly simpler method using a ramp and my router table. I simply position the work and the bit depth where I want the pocket to start. Then, keeping my hands well back from where the bit is, I plunge the piece onto the table and push it up the ramp until the bit quits cutting.

—VERNON TODD, *Springfield, Mo.*

Sliding Router Ramp for Pocket Holes

I BUILT THIS ROUTER-BASED POCKET-HOLE RAMP when I became frustrated with my drill pocket-hole fixture. The router slides down the ramps to cut a low 6°-angle pocket hole. It's quick and simple.

To make the fixture, attach two 6° ramps on each side of a plywood base. Install T-nuts and bolts in one of the ramps to provide a clamping system for the workpiece. Attach stops for the workpiece and the router at the base of the ramp. The distance between the router stop and the workpiece stop will determine the depth of the pocket hole, so position the stops carefully. Also, you will need to make an acrylic or Plexiglas base for your router. Add ¼-in.-thick guide rails to the underside of the base to ride on the outside of the ramps.

To set up for a cut, place the workpiece in the fixture against the stop, drop in some scrap spacers to hold the workpiece in position, then tighten the clamps. Chuck a ⅜-in. round-nose bit into the router. Turn the router on, and slide it down to the router stop to make the pocket hole. Drill the pilot hole in the pocket after the workpieces have been clamped together.

—MICHAEL CSONTOS, *Prescott, Ariz.*

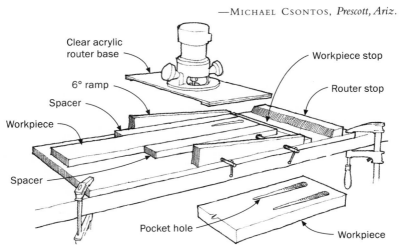

Clear acrylic router base

Workpiece stop

6° ramp

Router stop

Spacer

Workpiece

Spacer

Pocket hole

Workpiece

Routing European-Hinge Mortises

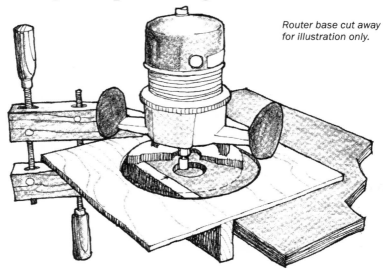

Router base cut away
for illustration only.

SEVERAL YEARS AGO, I remodeled my kitchen and painstakingly learned, through trial and error, many of the details for making European-style cabinets. I have neither a drill press nor the 1⅜-in. Forstner bit, which are commonly used to bore the large mortises for the door hinges. Instead, I made a router jig that did the job. To calculate the diameter of the cutout in the jig, add the router-base diameter to the mortise diameter, then subtract the diameter of the router bit. For example, if the diameter of the router base is 6 in., the mortise diameter 1⅜ in. and the router-bit diameter ½ in., the cutout diameter should be 6 in. plus 1⅜ in. minus ½ in., which equals 6⅞ in.

To rout the mortise, lock the jig in place with handscrews, lower the router base into the cutout, and move the router around and to and fro. To avoid overloading, especially with a light-duty router, make several passes, lowering the bit gradually to final depth.

—GRANT D. MILLER, *Reno, Nev.*

Routing Fingernail Edges

Y OUR ROUNDOVER ROUTER BITS can do double duty cutting
fingernail-shaped edges if you simply change the angle at which
the work moves into the bit. I use the bits in a router table with an
auxiliary fence that presents the stock to the bit at a 45° angle as illustrated. A ½-in. bit will mold the shape on ⅝-in.-thick stock, and a ¾-in.
bit will handle 1-in.-thick stock. Notice that the lip on the fence acts
as a track for the work and must have a gap in it so the bit can contact the work. For occasional use, this method beats buying the expensive specialty bit.

—JEFFREY P. GYVING, *Point Arena, Calif.*

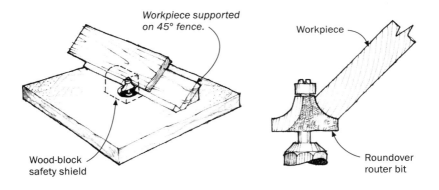

Workpiece supported
on 45° fence.

Workpiece

Wood-block
safety shield

Roundover
router bit

Trimming Edgebanding

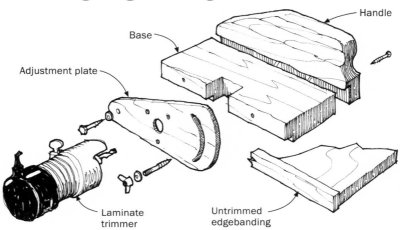

Handle

Base

Adjustment plate

Laminate
trimmer

Untrimmed
edgebanding

TRIMMING SOLID-WOOD EDGEBANDING on plywood with a plane
or belt sander can be a trying task, so I designed this simple
trimmer fixture, which holds a horizontally mounted router. An
adjustment mechanism allows the router's bit to be adjusted up or
down so it cuts the banding flush with the plywood. Instead of a full-
size router, I use a Porter-Cable laminate trimmer, which provides
plenty of power for trimming the ¼-in.- to ⅜-in.-thick banding I use.
I've found that an Onsrud ¼-in., two-flute spiral bit gives a smooth,
splinter-free cut that's ready for finish-sanding.

—WARREN W. BENDER, JR., *Medford, N.Y.*

Trimming Veneers

H ERE IS AN EASY AND CHEAP way to trim long edges of veneer. Make a guide from ¾-in. stock as long as the veneer, joint the edge straight and band with Formica. Put a lever-acting hold-down on each end of the guide board. Then set the veneer on the board, put a shorter piece of ¾-in. stock on top and tighten the hold-downs, as shown. Set the shaper or router cutter back ⅟₁₆ in. from the edge of the fence so that the cutter won't nick the edges of the guide boards as it trims the veneer. Trim with the grain of the veneer to prevent chipping, and be careful to hold onto the board. With this method I've joined veneers for 4-ft. by 10-ft. conference table tops with no problems.

—JIM SIEBURG, *Chicago, Ill.*

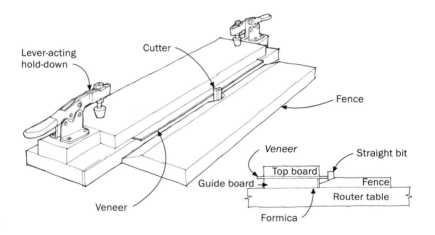

Making Fixed-Louver Shutters

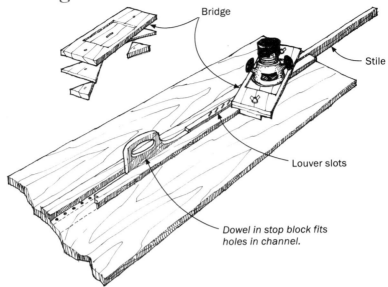

Bridge

Stile

Louver slots

Dowel in stop block fits holes in channel.

E XTERIOR WOOD REALLY TAKES A BEATING in the subtropical cli-
mate of Key West, Fl., where I work. So when a client hired our
company to replace his deteriorated pine shutters with longer-lasting
redwood, we developed this quick, easy and inexpensive method for
building the shutters right on the job site.

A tedious but critical part of shutter construction is routing slots in
the stiles for louvers. For this operation, we devised a jig, as shown in
the sketch, that holds the stile in a channel and allows it to be moved
in steps as each louver slot is routed. Accurate spacing is ensured by
using a stop block and a series of holes 1⅜ in. apart in the channel. A
dowel in the bottom of the stop block fits the holes. The jig is also fitted

with a bridge that holds the router above and at 18° to the stile. The bridge may be unfastened and repositioned to cut mirror-image slots in the mating stile. A recess in the top of the bridge allows the router to travel back and forth the precise distance needed to cut each slot.

To rout louver slots in a stile, we first mark off 6 in. at the top and bottom to allow enough room for the rails and waste. We also mark off the center of the stile where we skip two slots to leave room for the middle rail. Then, with the stile located in the jig's channel, we begin routing slots, tipping back the router to start the cut (a plunge router would be great for this job). After repositioning the bridge, we rout slots in the opposite stile. To complete the shutters, we mortise the stiles, cut tenons on the rails and glue up with epoxy and pipe clamps.

—BARB M. KAMM, *Key West, Fla.*

Producing Dollhouse Siding

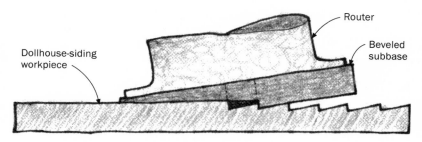

Router

Beveled
subbase

Dollhouse-siding
workpiece

H ERE'S HOW TO PRODUCE SIMULATED clapboard siding for doll-houses with a router and an easy-to-make subbase. First, to make the subbase, bevel a ¾-in. thick, 6-in. by 10-in. block on the tablesaw in much the same fashion as you would cut a raised panel. Be sure to leave a ⁄₁₆-in. or so fillet, as shown. Now bore a hole through the block, and mount the router so that a ¾-in. straight bit chucked in it is tangent to the fillet of the base. After experimenting with the bit depth, you should be able to rout multiple beveled cuts across the workpiece, indexing each cut in the previous cut. For narrower siding, relocate the subbase on the router and use either the same or a smaller bit.

—JIM AND DAN FORTNER, *Newport, Ind.*

Routing Tambour Grooves

I RECENTLY BUILT A SET OF DISPLAY CASES that had tamboured doors with ¼-in.-thick edges. I wanted the grooves in which they ran to be ½ in. wider so the tambour wouldn't bind. To accomplish this, I applied iron-on veneer edging tape around half the radius of my router base. To cut the groove, I ran the router base along a template using a ¼-in. straight bit. On the first pass, I kept the router's original base against the template. On the second pass, I rotated the router so the taped portion of the base bore against the pattern, thereby adding about ½ in. to the groove width.

—ANDREW DEY, *Wallingford, Conn.*

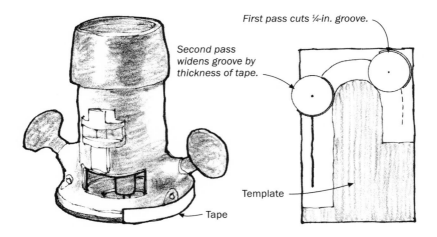

First pass cuts ¼-in. groove.

Second pass widens groove by thickness of tape.

Template

Tape

Coping Molding with a Router

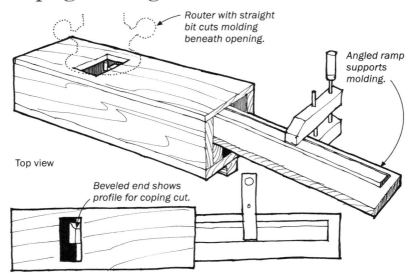

Router with straight bit cuts molding beneath opening.

Angled ramp supports molding.

Top view

Beveled end shows profile for coping cut.

A COPED JOINT FITS AND LOOKS BETTER than a mitered joint. So when I replaced all the base molding in my home, I decided to cope the joints at the inside corners of the rooms. Traditionally, joints are coped by first cutting a 45° miter on the end of one piece of molding, and then using a coping saw to cut along the curved line created where the miter cut intersects the molding's surface. This trims the end to the exact reverse section of the molding so that it will butt into the other piece of molding already installed tightly in the corner. Being fundamentally inept with hand tools, my attempts at sawing the joint fell far short of my expectations. Finally, I came up with the following router-based fixture, which makes this job more tolerable.

The fixture is a rectangular box with one open end, into which a wood ramp is inserted at a 20° angle. A rectangular hole is cut into the top of the box above the end of the ramp. A 2x4 attached to the bottom of the box enables the whole fixture to be clamped into a Work-Mate portable workbench. To use the fixture, cut the end of the molding at 45° so that the profile on the end shows the area to be coped away. Alternatively, you can scribe the molding with the shape to be cut and score any straight sections with a utility knife. In either case, insert the molding into the box and clamp it onto the ramp. Chuck a ³⁄₁₆-in. straight bit in a router, and insert the bit through the hole in the top of the fixture. Turn on the router and follow the scribed line to cut off the end of the molding. The angle of the ramp creates a slight back cut at the shaped edge, which makes the pieces fit together better. Before unclamping the workpiece, check the fit by inserting a short piece of molding through the top. Any necessary fine adjustments can be made with a file.

Once the molding is unclamped, the coped joint should fit quite well. After the first couple of tries, I became quite proficient with this system. The cuts were smooth, and the fit was better than anything I had previously achieved with a coping saw.

—SCOTT ASHWORTH, *Mars, Pa.*

Mounting Panels with Keyhole Slots

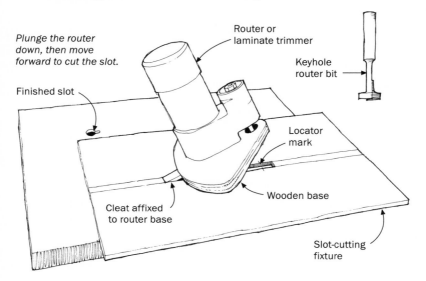

Plunge the router down, then move forward to cut the slot.

Router or laminate trimmer

Keyhole router bit →

Finished slot

Locator mark

Wooden base

Cleat affixed to router base

Slot-cutting fixture

A KEYHOLE ROUTER BIT CUTS A T-SHAPED SLOT that is useful for hanging picture frames. However, with a couple of simple fixtures, you can also use this bit to mount large panels flat to the wall. The benefits are many: The slots allow solid-wood panels to expand and contract; a damaged panel can easily be taken down, repaired and reinstalled; and there's no visible means of attachment, such as wires or nail holes.

To mount a panel with keyhole slots, you'll need a slot-cutting fixture and an alignment template. The alignment template is simply a piece of hardboard or plywood drilled with a pattern for mounting the screws. Attach the template to the wall, drill holes in the wall and insert pan-head screws, tightening them against a ¼-in.-thick scrap of wood to leave a consistent gap between the screw head and the wall. Transfer the template to the back of the panel, and mark each screw location.

To make the slot-cutting fixture, glue up several pieces of ¼-in.-thick material, leaving a ¾-in.-wide, 6-in.-long slot in the middle of the fixture (as shown in the sketch). To ride in that slot, make a ¾-in.-wide, 5½-in.-long maple cleat, drill a hole through one end of the cleat, then screw the cleat onto the bottom of your router base with the hole centered over the bit. (A wooden base added to your router makes this easier.) It is important that about 1 in. of the cleat hang over the edge of the router base to provide a lever arm for plunging the router. The cleat should slide freely in the slot.

Place the fixture on the back of the panel, aligning it with the screw-location marks, and clamp the fixture in place while you make your plunge cuts. You may need to adjust the depth of the screw heads on the wall for a perfect fit.

—TOM GRIFFIN, *Pleasanton, Calif.*

Registering Odd-Shaped Pieces

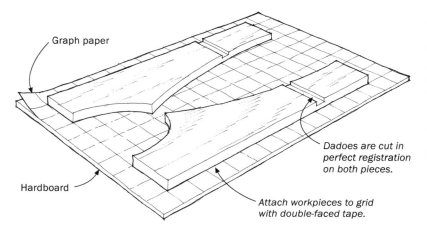

Graph paper

Hardboard

Dadoes are cut in
perfect registration
on both pieces.

Attach workpieces to grid
with double-faced tape.

H ERE IS A LITTLE TRICK that I discovered while making a display
shelf for my wife. With this technique, I was able to keep two
small, oddly shaped workpieces in exact registration to each other so
that I could rout dadoes in them. I began by mounting graph paper
on a squared-up piece of hardboard with spray adhesive. The grid lines
on the graph paper allowed me to position the shelf sides on the hardboard in perfect registration to each other. I attached the shelf sides to
the hardboard with double-faced carpet tape.

Finally, I flipped the whole thing upside down on the router table
and made my dado cuts by running the hardboard against the router-
table fence.

—DON DiPiero, *Girard, Ohio*

Routing the Edges of Odd-Shaped Pieces

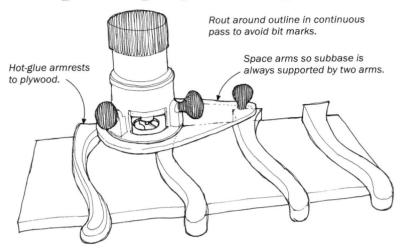

Rout around outline in continuous pass to avoid bit marks.

Hot-glue armrests to plywood.

Space arms so subbase is always supported by two arms.

S HAPING EDGES ON SMALL PIECES, such as rocking chair arms, with a router is always ticklish. Because I wanted to round over the perimeter in one pass to keep the cut smooth, I didn't want to clamp and reclamp each arm. Also, I needed to prevent the router from rocking on the small surface.

I solved the problem by hot-gluing all four armrests to a scrap piece of birch plywood, spaced 8 in. apart, in line and parallel. I used the extended subbase on my router supported by the adjacent armrest to steady the router. After shaping one side, I pried the armrests off and flipped them over to rout the other side.

It took only two little dabs of hot glue on each armrest to hold them. The dried glue, and occasional flakes of plywood veneer, were easily removed with a scraper. I've since used this technique successfully on other small parts where I needed a stable base and didn't want to spend a lot of time clamping and reclamping each piece.

—DAVE COUMES, *Franklin, Tenn.*

Routed Drawer Pull

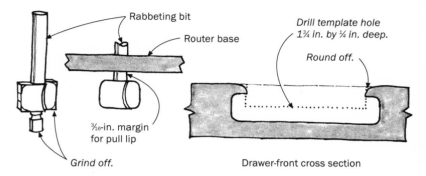

Rabbeting bit

Router base

Drill template hole
1¾ in. by ¼ in. deep.

Round off.

³⁄₁₆-in. margin
for pull lip

Grind off.

Drawer-front cross section

H ERE'S A SIMPLE AND VERSATILE DRAWER pull made with a modified router bit. Start with a small rabbeting bit (I used Stanley 82 150, which rabbets ¼ in. wide and ⁷⁄₁₆ in. deep). Grind off the pilot and round the corners, taking care not to lose the correct bevel. Chuck the bit in the router with the cutter about ³⁄₁₆ in. below the base.

Next drill or rout a template hole in the drawer front. I use a 1¾-in. multispur bit, boring to a depth of only ¼ in. so the bit's pilot hole will later be removed. A flat-bottomed Forstner bit would be better because it leaves no pilot hole. If you use a straight router bit, you can cut any shape template hole.

Now plunge the router with the modified bit into the center of the template hole and work it out to the edge, using the bit's shank to guide (apply paraffin) against the side of the template hole. Finish the pull by rounding the top with a reverse-curve spoon gouge.

—MILES KARPILOW, *Emeryville, Calif.*

Drilling Adjustable-Shelf Pinholes

THE BEST WAY TO DRILL ADJUSTABLE-SHELF PINHOLES in cabinets is with a ¼-in. bit in a plunge router. This is especially true for materials like melamine. You'll need a guide with holes to fit the router's template guide. Polycarbonate, ¼ in. thick, is a good choice for the pinhole guide.

For my guide, I used a drill press to make ⅞₆-in. holes (to match the diameter of my router's template guide) on 1½-in. centers. On one end of the template, write "top" so when you are setting up to bore holes in the workpiece, you can orient the template the same way.

To use, clamp the template along one edge of the cabinet with spring clamps and two pieces of double-faced tape. Then plunge the router in all of the pilot holes. When you are finished with one side, flip the template, and move it to the other edge, making sure "top" is at the top of the cabinet.

—L. L. CHIP LUTZ, *Puyallup, Wash.,*
and Leslie O. Payne, Gaston, Ore.

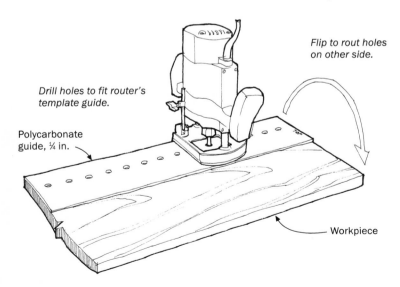

Flip to rout holes
on other side.

Drill holes to fit router's
template guide.

Polycarbonate
guide, ¼ in.

Workpiece

Chucking Bowl Blanks

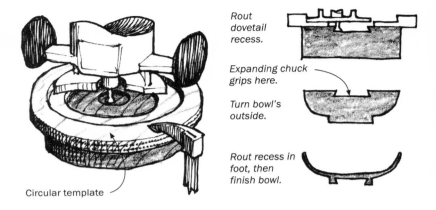

Rout dovetail recess.

Expanding chuck grips here.

Turn bowl's outside.

Rout recess in foot, then finish bowl.

Circular template

I T SEEMS TO ME, IN READING PAST METHODS on woodturning, that many turners must be spending more time fiddling with faceplates and attaching the work to the lathe than actually turning. I'd rather spend my time turning, so I devised this quick procedure that takes me from a blank to a finished 10-in.-dia. bowl with ⅛-in.-thick walls in 30 minutes.

The key to the method is a 6-in-1 universal chuck, which has an expanding collet that locks into a dovetail recess in the workpiece. First I cut a recess in the top of the blank, using a router with a dovetail bit and the circular template shown in the sketch. The router rides around inside the shoulder on the template to produce a recess to fit the chuck.

With the circular blank mounted on the chuck, I turn the bowl's outside profile. At this point you can turn a chuck recess in the bottom of the bowl if you choose, but I find it easier and faster to remove the bowl and cut the new recess with the router. It's important to center the bowl's foot in the template before cutting the recess, otherwise the bowl will wobble on the lathe. If you turn the foot to fit the center hole in the template, this won't be a problem.

Now I return the bowl to the lathe and complete the inside. If desired, you can part off the bowl above the foot to eliminate all signs of the attachment method.

—F. H. CREWS, *High Point, N.C.*

Routing Wooden Spheres

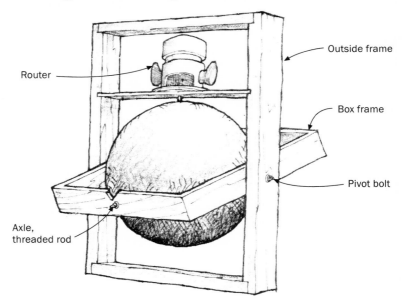

Router

Outside frame

Box frame

Pivot bolt

Axle,
threaded rod

L AST CHRISTMAS, I WANTED TO GIVE MY WIFE a sphere covered
with ½-in.-sq. mirrors. Styrofoam was my first thought, but a plastic ball would have cost $32, so I decided to make one from wood and
devised this simple router fixture to do it.

First, glue up a rough sphere by laminating graduated discs of plywood or solid wood; the larger discs should be rings, to save weight
and material. Drill a hole through the north and south poles so that
the blank can be mounted on a threaded-rod axle inside a box frame,
as shown in the sketch. Washers serve as shims to center the blank in
the frame.

The outside frame is just wider than the box frame, which pivots inside it on two mounting bolts. The sphere should rotate smoothly within the box frame; the box frame should turn smoothly within the outside frame.

Center a router on a platform so that the bit is suspended over the sphere.

To rout the sphere, first clamp the fixture to the bench. Then rotate the rough sphere to find its high spot, and set the router bit a little lower than this. Turn on the router and rotate the sphere inside the box frame, occasionally pivoting the box frame a little within the outside frame. Continue lowering the router bit until the sphere is true. Except for a small area at each pole, the router bit can reach every point on the sphere. The small flat spots at the poles can easily be rounded off by hand.

—FRANK D. HART, *Plainfield, Ind.*

INDEX

A

Arcs:
  along beam, sled for, 191
  jigs for, 160–63
Armoire, molded corner edge for, 186–87

B

Bases:
  asymmetrical, making, 58–59, 86
  eccentric,
    making, 70–71, 85
    using, 85
  extension, 68
  mounting onto, 21
  see-through, 59
  sub-, making, 61
  truing, 19
Beams, rounding, sled for, 191
Bearings, Delrin-sleeved, 199
Bedposts, jig for, 183–85
Bending: See Forms
Biscuit joinery: See Plate joinery
Bits:
  beading, 187
  care of, 11, 15
  cleaning, 18–19
  collars for vs. ball-bearing, 6–7
  for finger joints, 137
  flush-trimming, 6
  glue-joint, aligning, 132
  height-adjusting, aid for, 55
  for jointing, 130
  making, 31
  panel-raising, 202
  for plastic laminate, 199
  protecting, 49
  quality, choosing, 11

shaper, in routers, 22–23
sizes of, and cut, 7, 22–23
slippage of, preventing, 16–17
spiral-flute, 7
stagger-tooth, 168
for tearout reduction, 7
two vs. three, 7
See also Sharpening; Speed; Steel; Storage
Bowls:
  chuck recesses for, 228–29
  recessing, 164–67
Box joints: See Finger joints.
Burning, causes of, 28

C

Circles:
  guides for, 156–59, 168–70, 212
  See also Arcs.
Collets, cleaning, 19
Columns, fluting, jig for, 174–75
Coping, setup for, 220
Countertops, radiusing, 160–63
Cylinders:
  tapered, 208
  See also Dowels.

D

Dadoes:
  cutting, safely, 84
  enlarging, 85
  jigs for, 74–75, 78–81, 84–88, 124–25
  laying out,
    board for, 66–67
    procedure for, 76
  matching, in odd-shaped pieces, 224
  tongues for, cutting, 82–83, 89

Depth settings:
  choosing, 28
  with drill bits, 26
Dovetails:
  bushings for, reworking, 29
  cutting, 94–95
  fit of, perfecting, 29
  jigs for, improving, 97
  sliding,
    double, 107
    jigs for, 101–106
    for pedestal legs, 108–109
  templates for, 92, 95
  trimming, 100
  waste removal for, 96–99
Dowels, making, 204–206
Drawers:
  fronts of, tearout prevention for, 196–98
  joinery for, 140–41
  pulls for, 226
  with sliding dovetails, 106
Drill presses, as router mounts, 52
Duplicating, on lathe, router jig for, 207
Dust collection, attaching, 25

E

Edgebanding:
  applying, 62–63
  trimming, 62–63, 214
  See also Moldings
Edge-rounding:
  of odd shapes, 225
  setup for, 69

F

Fences:
  angled, for edging discs, 54

blade-guard and stop, 51
for edge-banding, 62–63
flip-up, 87
for molding trimming, 64–65
purfling, 60
setting, 20
scissor-jack, 45
Finger joints:
clean, method for, 137
jigs for, 134–35, 136
Flutes, jigs for, 174–77
Forms, curved, making, 171
Frames, circular segmented, jointing, 151

G

Grooves:
angled, jigs for, 144–45, 147–50
keyhole, 222–23
setup for, 180
for shutter louvers, 216–17
square tapered, 178
stopped, 180–82
tambour, 219
V-, in tongue-and-groove stock, 179
See also Dadoes
Guides:
for circles, 156–59, 168–70
with clamp and channel, 80
commercial, 80, 84
for shelf-pin holes, 227
from T-squares, 77
See also Dadoes; individual operations

I

Inlay, stopped grooves for, 181–82

J

Jigs, mounting onto, 21

Joinery: See Dadoes; Dovetails; Finger joints; Mortises; Plate joinery; Scarf joints; Splines; Tongue-and-rabbet joints
Jointing:
with glue-joint bit, 132
methods for, 130–31, 133
of mitered segments, 151
of veneer, 215
See also Planing.

L

Laminate trimmer:
dovetail cleanup with, 98–99
for edgebanding, 214
Legs:
fluting, jig for, 174–75
grooves in, square tapered, 178
reeding, jig for, 183–85
sliding dovetails for, 108–109
Log slabs, surfacing, 193

M

Milling, of tree section, from door setup, 192–93
Miters:
plate joinery for, 143–45
splined, jigs for, 141, 146, 147–50
Moldings:
applied, trimming, 64
on carcase edge, 186–87
coping, jig for, 220
fingernail, setup for, 213
making, 170
See also Panels, raising
Mortisers, horizontal, jigs for, 113, 115–16
pivoting, 118–20
Mortises:
centering, 126–27
deep, 117

hinge, 124–25
European, 212
jigs for, 112, 114–15, 121
adjustable, 122–23
two-plane, 113
multiple, jig for, 142

P

Panels:
keyhole mounting slots for, 222–23
raising, jigs for, 200–203
tearout prevention for, 196–98
Pin routers:
on drill presses, 52
on radial-arm saws, 53
Planing:
jig for, 190
sleds for, 188–89
thicknessing, jig for, 190
See also Milling
Plastic laminate:
lubricant for, 199
trimming, without scratching, 199
Plate joinery:
method for, 138–39, 144
for miters, jigs for, 143–45
Plunge routing, makeshift, 24
Pocket holes, jigs for, 209–211
Pulls, drawer, 226
Purfling, guide for, 60

R

Radial-arm saws, as router mounts, 53
Reeding, jigs for, 183–85

S

Scarf joints:
curved, method for, 135
in plywood, jig for, 152
Screws: See Pocket holes
Shapers, vs. routers, 22

Sharpening:
with diamond hone, 8
indications for, 10
Shelves, pin holes for, 227
Shutters, fixed-louver, slots
for, 216–17
Siding, for dollhouse, 218
Speed, for large bits, 12
Spheres, truing, setup for,
230–31
Splines:
corner, jig for, 136
in miters, 141, 146,
147–50
Steel:
high-speed vs. carbide-
tipped, 8
titanium-nitride coated,
9
Storage:
drawer for, under-
bench, 14
in foam, 15
trays for, grommeted, 13

T

Tables:
bench-remountable, 40
circles on, 159
extension base for, 68
horizontal-vertical
combination, 37
inserts for, adjustable, 41
knockdown, 39
mounting onto, 21
mounts for, toggle-
clamp, 48–49, 50
plunge routers in, 44
disadvised, 43–44
lifts for, 46–47, 50
routers for, 43
switches for, toggle, 42
from tablesaw outfeed,
34
on tablesaw stands, 35,
36, 38
tenons on, 153
Tablesaws, and router
tables, 34–35
removable, 36

Tabletops:
radiusing, 160–63
recessing, 164–67
Tambours, grooves for, 219
Tearout:
avoiding, 27
and bits, 7
cleaning up, 27
on drawer fronts,
preventing,
196–98
Template routing:
bits for, 6
See also Dovetails,
templates for
Tenons, round, on router
table, 153
Tongue-and-groove, V-
grooves for, 179
Tongue-and-rabbet joints,
method for,
140–41
Tongues, cutting, 82–83,
89
Toys:
dollhouses, siding for,
218
tearout prevention for,
198

V

Veneer:
jointing, 215
See also Edgebanding